TORODE'S
THAI TREK

Acknowledgements

It is not every day that you are asked to travel around and write a book about a country that you find fascinating. For the privilege, there are a few people I need to thank.

Helen Williams, who was mad enough to commission the series and use me as the front man and who continues to keep me on my toes and Nicky Paris, the only editor who could put up with the continuous stream of guff that I produced. You are both mad and that's why we get on so well. Much love.

The production team in Thailand: Sophie, who goes down as the star of the journey for soldiering on with motion and sea sickness when trains, planes and boats were part of our every day life. It did give us a giggle. And the two bestest camera men – one of whom had to do sound – Jason and Kym. Thanks for the insect repellent in the form of consumed alcohol. I hope you like the pictures. Thank you all.

And of course, my beautiful wife Angie and wonderful boys Marcel and Casper, for letting me pursue food, cooking and all the joys that go with it.
John Torode

TORODE'S
THAI TREK
JOHN TORODE

THIS morning

GRANADA
MEDIA

Torode's Thai Trek was produced for transmission on Granada TV's *This Morning* programme, September 1999

Presented by John Torode
Producer: Fiona MacAskill
Director: Sophie Hodgekins
Series Editor: Helen Williams

First published in 1999 by Granada Media
an imprint of André Deutsch Limited
in association with Granada Media Group
76 Dean Street
London
W1V 5HA
www.vci.co.uk

ISBN 0 233 99649 4

Design by Carroll Associates
Printed and bound in the UK by Jarrold Book Printing

CONTENTS

INTRODUCTION

'The Land of Smiles'. This is how many of us have come to know Thailand, and it is the way in which the people who inhabit this wonderful country like it to be recognized. They are the friendliest and the most helpful of people. And when it comes to learning about their food, there are many men, women and children who are all extremely willing and eager to teach inquisitive people like me.

Not many of us get the chance to travel a country from top to bottom on a culinary expedition. On my trek through Thailand, I took every advantage to soak up new information and to re-affirm and hone the skills and knowledge that I already had. The sheer beauty of Thailand is hard for people who haven't been there to comprehend. Many different cultural influences have contributed to the way Thailand is today. It has a chequered political past, with everything from kings who were greatly loved by the people to unwanted dictators and invading forces, but throughout all this, the people of Thailand have remained friendly and courteous to visitors to their country.

Respect is important as it is in many other cultures. If you don't play by the rules then things are not as easy as they should or could be. In Western culture we usually expect our children to treat adults with respect and address them as Mr or Mrs; in Thailand the equivalent title is Khun. There is no gender difference; it is the same for male and female. But knowing this made life easier for me and meant that I was able to communicate properly with many more people as the journey progressed.

Our trek covered most of the country. At the start, I really got a taste for the high life travelling aboard the 'Eastern Oriental Express'. It took three days and two nights and numerous bottles of champagne to do the 2,000 kilometre train journey from Singapore to Bangkok. After I stepped off the train in Bangkok, one of my very favourite places, I started to talk to people and understand more clearly the culture that I was in. From there I travelled a further 2,500 kilometres by land, river, sea and plane going as far north as the Burmese border. Then I went all the way back down to the border of Malaysia and toured the beautiful islands off Thailand's east coast. This, incidentally, is where Alex Garland's novel *The Beach* is set.

If you don't have some understanding of a country's cultural past, I do not feel you can do justice to its cuisine. Fundamental to any understanding of Thai food is the concept of balance. As Buddhism is the religion of the majority of the population, it plays a large part in life as a whole. Thais, like the Chinese, believe in balance and for Thai food to be considered great, it needs harmony. In the West we use flavours and textures to produce harmony in certain food combinations without even realizing it. For example, tomato with basil, mozzarella and olive oil – simple but perfect. As for texture,

The most vital element in Thai food – rice.

a good example would be bangers and mash. Harmony as it applies to Thai food, however, is somewhat different. There are four elements that make up this balance: sweet, sour, salty and hot. The way these are perceived has all to do with the way that food is tasted in Thailand, and tasting Thai food is very different from the way we taste food in the West. We Westerners are not taught how to taste and this does inhibit our ability to cook.

When tasting Thai food, certain areas in the mouth should react to different flavours – sweet at the front of the tongue and sour at the back, salt on the cheeks and heat in the back of the throat. To judge whether the food you taste is balanced, you should feel that none of the areas mentioned are affected any more than any other, and that the sensation of flavour and taste fills the whole mouth. As with Western food, seasoning can be adjusted and you can increase or decrease the sensation of heat. For instance, if a green curry is too hot, then add some more palm sugar as the sweetness will take away the burning heat. If you would like it to be slightly hotter, then add some fish sauce as this will help to bring out the heat. The four elements of sweet, sour, salty and hot exist in many single dishes but not in all; some may only have three, such as the three-flavour sauce. But as a rule the four elements should exist in a main meal where many different dishes are all served at once and where cooks like me get the chance to really show off.

In Thailand, the main family meal and all those meals prepared for special occasions are composed of a great variety of dishes. These may include soup, salad, a curry or three, a number of nam priks and relishes, sometimes a plain omelette to go with the curry and of course the most vital element of all, rice. The Thai phrase for eating is kin khao, which literally translates as 'to eat rice', which shows how important

8

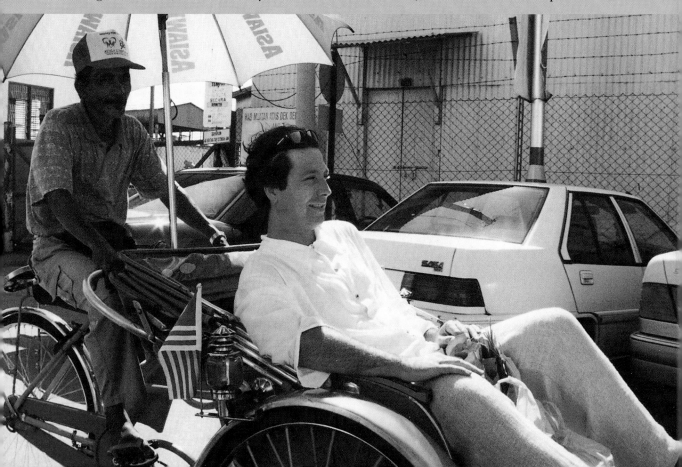

The ever versatile wok. Thais use this for everything – from frying to boiling and steaming.

rice really is. As a poor nation, rice has been the staple diet of Thailand for many centuries and many different types of rice are grown in different regions. The correct ratio of rice to other foods should be 10:1, however because of our wealth in the West, we tend to serve one part of rice to every ten parts of other food.

Rice also helps draw the heat from other food and that is maybe why many Thai people can cope so much better with the chilli than us. Rice is sacred and should never be wasted. For breakfast, many Thais eat Khao Tom (rice soup) made of good stock, rice, seasoning and coriander leaves which is then spiced up with Nam Pla (fish sauce with chillies). Sticky rice has always been served with meals as it absorbs the sauce and is easy for people to eat with their fingers. Then, about fifty years ago, a dictator named Phibul decreed that everybody must eat with a fork and a spoon. There are two reasons why knives do not appear on the table. First, this is because all Thai food is cut into small pieces before it is cooked and therefore there is no need to cut anything at the table. Secondly, if anybody places a knife on a table whilst people are eating, it will be taken as a threat of violence because a knife is considered a weapon.

Red meat has not been part of Thai cuisine for very long. Early and ancient Buddhists believed that animals should not be slaughtered for food so the only time that the flesh of red meat was made available was after a sacrifice to the gods. Fish, chickens and shellfish have always been used in abundance. Precisely what an individual Thai person will and will not eat is largely dictated by region. Southerners exist largely on a diet of coconuts and sea fish, both plentiful in the South. The inhabitants of the central plains take their food from the many rivers, or 'klongs' as they are known, feeding on everything from large fresh water fish, eels, crustaceans, small turtles and even the

Thai people spend many therapeutic hours preparing their food.

occasional frog. Chickens are obviously important to the rural, farming regions, not to mention the egg. The North also utilizes its rivers but has the added advantage of a jungle full of birds and other wild beasts. It is also the rice capital of the country. These rice fields produce land crabs, which are small but very strong in flavour and great when eaten with a classic Som Tum (green papaya salad).

It is, however, interesting that many Thai people do not cook every day but often get a take away. This is particularly true of the more populated areas, especially in and around Bangkok Klongs. From long boats many men and women sell raw produce, but they also often have facilities for cooking which enable them to sell a range of wonderful snacks and noodles direct as they drift by. These people must have been the model for the original travelling sales person and surely the oldest home delivery service!

The other location that is one of the most popular for eating and socializing in Thailand is the street. Street food across the whole of the country has to be amongst the most underrated food in the world. Many visitors are scared and find it hard to believe that some of the best food comes from the street. Stallholders specialize in particular aspects of Thai food, and are well patronized by the people who live and work in that area. It is not a tourist gimmick as these traders cannot afford to offer food of a poor quality – quite simply it is their livelihood. Everything is served off these stalls – from bowls of noodles, which are always served as a snack and the only thing eaten with chopsticks, to the famous green papaya salad which is pounded in front of you, to which you can specify how much chilli you want to add.

A stall off the Sukinvit road where fishcakes are cooked, is so busy in the morning that they have six people working at it, and the only job of one woman is to drop these

Measuring spoon, cooking spoon, stirrer and taster.

quick-frying, spongy, spiced pieces of fish into the fat. The people of Thailand don't eat three meals a day like us but continually snack, eating up to six times a day but sometimes making do with just a bowl of rice. As a culture they are frugal and this means that the food they cook can contain the same plant in varying forms. In a crispy noodle salad, the lime is used in three different ways; the juice is used for the dressing, the rind for part of the salad and the leaf to garnish. The banana tree is also put to several different uses. Its leaves are used for decoration and as a wrapping for fish to flavour it when grilled over embers, and the flowers of the plant are treated in the same way as we treat artichokes and are used in salads. When ripe, the banana itself is eaten both raw and cooked, and it is also sometimes cooked in sugar syrup when still green.

Food is a huge part of the daily routine in Thailand. As most families go to the market early in the morning to collect the daily produce, it seems as though the entire day is taken up with various different rituals to do with food. The whole family pitches in and the mother teaches all Thai children from an early age how to use a pestle and mortar. The use of the pestle and mortar means that the flesh of the plant is broken at a natural seam allowing the natural oils to be released. There's no right way; many people pound straight down and then push the food back into the base with a spoon, others pound on the side; the only thing that seems to be standard is to put in only small amounts at a time.

Much time is spent over the preparation of Thai food and cooking times may seem quite short by comparison. Actually, as I have become more involved, even the mundane jobs, such as the peeling of the shallots and the pounding in a pestle and mortar, have become therapeutic. Perhaps the best way to look on this preparation time is to see it as the beginning of a great ceremony, in which everything has its natural place and works in harmony with everything else. In the end, it all seems to come back to respect for a culture quite different to our own. We can learn about many other things if we decide to study how to cook Thai food and I have been lucky enough to start on that journey.

BASIC INGREDIENTS

Lemon Grass (tak rai)

This wild grass is the most commonly known Thai flavour. It is long and thin like all wild grass and can be grown in home gardens that have plenty of sun to help develop its flavour. Both the inner and the outer casing are used in Thai dishes. The inner case is soft enough to be used for pastes and is sliced thinly. The outer case is used to flavour soups and sauces. Lemon grass is also used to make tea; boiling water can be poured over the trimmings from the day's cooking and left to infuse. Lemon grass is also used by some cooks as a spoon; the base is bruised and the rest placed in the pot to act as the stirrer and a flavouring agent.

Galangal (kai)

This rhizome, or thick-stemmed plant, is the sister to ginger and is also known by the name 'greater ginger'. Galangal should, at its best, be pink in colour, and have stems attached. As it gets older, the skin will turn white with brown strips. It has a powerful aniseed flavour and is spicy hot to eat. Like ginger, it is usually peeled first and is used in everything from soups to paste, but unlike ginger, it is rarely used in salads as it is most often cooked to release all the flavours.

Lime Leaf (makrut)

From the Kaffir lime tree, to me these leaves are an important symbol of food in Thailand. Piled up in huge mountains in the markets in Bangkok, bound in handfuls with nylon, they still have their stems attached. You should take care as the stems have very sharp thorns. Lime leaves are used in a variety of ways; the potent, spicy flavour is released by tearing the leaves, which can be put in curries and soups, or crushed in noodles, or sliced thinly in salad. Most supermarkets sell lime leaves dried or you can also buy them frozen.

Snake Beans (thua fak yao)

Known by many names in English, including 'long bean' and 'yard-long beans', these are nuttier than the string or French bean. About 50-60cm long in bundles held together with a rubber band, these beans do not lend themselves very well to being boiled as we might cook them the UK. Instead they are fried with stir fries and pad phriks, or served raw with relishes and nam phriks.

Thai Shallots (hom lek)

Thai shallots are small and red in colour. They are tiresome to peel and at times you wonder why they are used in preference to the larger versions. It is all about the difference in flavour; the Thai shallot is sweet, contains a lot of sugar and is not as acidic as the large shallot, meaning that it can be eaten raw in salads as well as being used in curries. To deep fry shallots to make a crisp garnish, put the sliced shallots in oil that is just warm and increase the heat. This way the water will evaporate before the sugar turns to caramel and the shallots will become golden and crisp. If they turn dark and floppy, this means that the oil was too hot and they will taste bitter like overcooked caramel.

Chillies (phrik)

There are many types of chilli used in Thai cooking, from the long red chilli known as the serrano to the very small chilli called phrik khi nu, which, due to its size, is literally translated as rat droppings. Chilli comes from the capsicum family and the more mature the chilli, the more deep red in colour it will be. These deep red chillies are dried in the sun and then pounded to make chilli powder. They are also used as the base for pad phriks or curry pastes once they are re-hydrated. The seeds of all chillies are the part of the plant that gives off the most heat, but that is not to say that the flesh is not hot also.Wear protective gloves when preparing lots of chillies and always wash your hands in cold water because hot water will open up the pores of the skin and may cause burns.

Pandan (bai toey)

The pandanus bush is a grass not unlike pampas grass. It grows well in warm shaded spots and is found in Thai gardens under banana trees. The long, thin leaf is used only as flavouring and is not edible. Pandan leaves have a nutty and woody flavour and are used to wrap chicken (see Minced Chicken in Pandan on page 58), protecting the delicate chicken meat as well as giving flavour. They can also be used when cooking sweet things, to flavour rice and coconut milk. Banana leaf can be substituted but it will need first to be first dropped into hot water to make it more flexible. Some Thai supermarkets sell frozen pandan leaves.

Thai Basil (horapha)

Also known in Thailand as sweet basil, its leaves are a rich shade of green and are tinged with purple. The stems also have purple running through them. Thai basil is shiny, has a very short shelf life and, as it does not like moisture, is best stored wrapped in paper in a cool place. Its flavour is stronger then the Italian variety, being highly perfumed with aniseed. Use in small amounts as it can very quickly overpower a dish.

Coriander (pak chee)

Known as cilantro in America, this fast-growing herb with frilly leaves is a member of the carrot family and its popularity is increasing at a rapid rate. The whole coriander plant, including the roots, has a function; the leaves for garnishing, the stems for flavouring and the roots once scraped and crushed can also be used for flavouring. An alternative to coriander pak chee, pak chee farang, is a herb used mainly in the North and it is also known by the name 'pak chee loas'. It grows in dry soil in small patches and its leaves are long and thin and look like the nose of a swordfish. Unlike the coriander plant, the root of this plant cannot be used at all. The leaves are shredded for salads and are used as a garnish.

Peppercorns (phrik thai)

Peppercorns are available in Thailand in two different forms. The fresh green peppercorn, sometimes available on stems in supermarkets, look, in their young and fresh state, like little green berries on a highly textured branch. As peppercorns mature, they turn a darker shade of green and when dried, they turn black. Thais never make use of the black peppercorn. Instead they peel off the outer black casing and polish the inside until it is magically revealed as a white peppercorn. Pepper is important to Thai cuisine because prior to Portuguese traders arriving and introducing chillies, the peppercorn was the main source of heat in food.

Kaffir Lime (makrut)

The fruit of the Kaffir tree is very different to the lime that is familiar worldwide. The outer skin is knobbly and rough in appearance, the pith is thick and, like the normal lime the juice, is sour, but the Kaffir tastes rather strange because of its hot, spicy flavour which is highly perfumed like the leaves. The rind is used to flavour curries and the juice for dressings and for finishing off soups when the balance needs to be made a little sourer.

Green Mustard (phak kwang)

The green mustard plant looks similar to a cabbage, but with longer bright green leaves which are not so tightly clumped. The leaves have a thick hefty texture and are oval in shape and the stem is thick and can be cooked. Its flavour, as the name suggests, is hot like mustard and is not dissimilar in taste to the Japanese plant wasabi.

Water Chestnut (haeo)

Available mainly in cans, water chestnuts can be bought fresh at certain times of year in Chinese supermarkets. The best time to buy these small black tubers is Chinese New Year. The outer skin needs to be removed once they have been boiled, revealing the off-white crunchy, nutty flesh inside.

1. Green Mustard Leaf
2. Bok Choy
3. Bananas
4. Lemon Grass
5. Thai Shallots
6. Green Mango
7. Assorted Chillies
8. Coconut
9. Snake Beans
10. Garlic
11. Galangal
12. Green Bananas
13. Water Chestnuts
14. Coriander
15. Young Coconut
16. Green Papaya
17. Thai Basil
18. Gourd
19. Pandan Leaf
20. Choy Sum
21. Lime Leaf
22. Chinese Chives
23. Coriander Leaf

Chinese Chives (ton kra-thiam)
Also known as the garlic leaf, these long-thin leaves smell highly of garlic at their best and of bad feet when they are past their prime. There are two types available; bright green and shiny white; the white ones are grown in the dark and the flavour is quite bitter. I prefer the green version.

Rice (khao jao)
Rice is the staple food of the Thais. The word for rice, 'kin khao', means 'to eat' in Thai, which shows just how important rice is to this country. Rice in the central and southern areas of Thailand the most popular rice is long grain, non-glutinous rice. In its raw state it is highly polished and translucent; only when it is cooked does it become white and fluffy.

Glutinous Rice (khao niao)
This is the rice preferred in the North and it is the mainstay of this poorer region. Also known as sticky rice, its grains are once again highly polished, but are chalky rather than translucent, indicating a high level of starch. This rice is used also by Thais in the cooking of sweet dishes such as sticky rice and banana. Glutinous rice is grown in many varieties in various different locations, ranging from the rice grown on the flat and terraced paddy field to the wild land rice grown by the hill tribes in the furthest northern areas close to Burma.

Pot Crust (khao tang)
This is the rice crust that forms at the bottom of the cooking pot. Dried in the sun, it becomes crisp and smoky in flavour and is eaten with a nam phrik or lom. It is sold as a snack in markets in Thailand.

18

Roast Rice (kao krua)
Roast rice is used as a garnish and as texture for salads such as larps. The rice should be soaked in water for one hour and the excess water drained off before it is placed on a baking sheet. It should then be roasted in a moderate oven for 20 minutes until coloured, left to cool and pounded into small pieces.

Rice Noodle (kuai tiao)
The flat noodle, part of the famous Phad Thai dish, can be bought fresh in Thailand, but only dry in this country. They are available in three different widths; sen yai (2-3cm wide), sen lek (5mm) and the thinnest sen mi (1-2mm). Made from rice flour and water, the mix is rolled out and left to dry in the sun and then cut. Before cooking the dry noodles need to be re-hydrated. A large bowl should be filled with water at room temperature and the noodles dropped into it. This should be left for one hour and the water then drained off.

Rice Vermicelli (khanom jin)
Also made of rice, these noodles are not flat as kuai tiao, but are round and very fine. They are chalky in the dry state and translucent when re-hydrated. Vermicelli are used in many dishes including raw in salads, and as part of a sweet dish such as rice noodles in coconut milk. They can also be deep-fried as the base of candied noodles, and used as a garnish for dishes such as Chiang Mai noodle.

Oil Noodles

The white thick noodles, known as 'udon' in most supermarkets, are made of flour and water and are coated with oil to stop them from sticking together. They also have some not-too-distant cousins that are yellow and used for stir-frying with egg.

Ming Noodles

These Chinese yellow egg noodles can be bought fresh and dried in Thailand. When dried, they look similar to a small bird's nest. Boil them before using in soups and curries and they should not be used for stir frying.

Palm Sugar (nam tan pip)

Called 'nam tan pip' in Thailand, the sugar was originally extracted from the sugar palm known as 'tan'. Some sugar is still extracted from these palms, but most of it is now taken from the coconut palm, which is also referred to as coconut sugar. It is sold in Thailand in 5 litre (8¾ pints) petrol containers called pips. Now sold in many forms from the easy-to-use and convenient tablets to the not-so-easy-to-use jars, it is used in various dishes such as curries, desserts and the wonderful nam Jim.

Tamarind (makam sot or bliak)

This thick, seeded paste is taken from the dried pod of the tamarind tree. The pod is similar to a broad bean but smaller. Tamarind is sold in supermarkets in block form, where the outer pod has been removed and the flesh of several beans are pressed together. It is usually mixed with water, and then used as a souring agent in Thai dishes. To make the water, equal quantities of the pulp should be placed in a bowl with warm water and then massaged. The water will turn brown and the flavour will be sour. If the mixture is left to rest for 10 minutes, the water will thicken. To make thin water the process should be repeated once the first lot of water has been used.

Fish Sauce (nam pla)

Fish sauce is liquid salt in its true and refined form. It has been around for centuries, with the Romans using it at the time they invaded England. Made from the fermented juice that is brought about by mixing fish, usually anchovies, with shrimps and salt; it is then left in the sun to ferment and the liquid is drained off. Fish sauce is sold in bottles in this country and in plastic jugs in Thailand. Used as a condiment on every table and as the salt agent in all Thai food, the smell of less good fish sauce is pungent but sweet. I would recommend buying a Thai brand rather than a Malay or Vietnamese, as the flavour is more well rounded, and soft rather than harsh.

Shrimp Paste (ka-pi)

Many people find this Thai ingredient rather off-putting because of its strange smell. Chances are, there will come a time when both fish sauce and shrimp paste smell heavenly, as it is a signal that good food is not far away. The paste is made by mixing small prawns with salt and leaving them to ferment. Then the mixture is pounded into a paste. Once again it is sweet in flavour, well rounded and a pinkish red colour. The Thai paste is again different from Malay paste as it is black, sticky and very strong. Sold in both tubs and in small blocks, shrimp paste is tasty as a nam phrik and can be wrapped in banana leaf and roasted over coals or added to food as a condiment.

19

Essential flavours

1. Small Chillies
2. Large Chilli (serrano)
3. Lime Leaf
4. Lemon Grass
5. Thai Shallots
6. Thai Basil
7. Coriander
8. Garlic
9. Galangal
10. Snake Beans
11. Mint

Dried Shrimps (kung haeng)

These little dried shrimps have many different uses. They can be used as flavouring in pastes and dressing, pounded for flavour, included as texture in papaya salad or fried in Phat Thai. Thai markets are full of stalls selling big mountains of dried shrimps but the quality of the shrimp varies greatly. In this country they are sold in small bags, and the best ones to use are those that are natural pink and white, as the bright ones have been dyed with food colouring and are stuffed with E numbers.

Dark Soy (nam siew)

Remembering that soy is basically a Chinese condiment, the dark soy is not seen very often in Thai recipes. It is made by fermenting soya beans with salt in a large barrel in the sun, although these days the fermentation is more likely to take place in a large factory. Dark soy should be thick and sweet. The Malaysian version is called ketchup manis, as used in Noodles and Bean Shoots with Sweet Soy(see page 42).

Light Soy (man siew)

Light soy is used in Thai food in the same way as fish sauce, if the fish sauce bottle runs low, Thai light soy can be used as a substitute. Different from the Japanese version, Thai soy is very thin and brown in colour rather than dark black.

Oyster Sauce (nam man hoi)

Thick sweet, soy is flavoured with oyster extract to make this versatile sauce. The major problem with oyster sauce seems to be that the brands you can buy in the supermarket are often too thick or too salty. Good Thai oyster sauce does not contain MSG and it is important therefore to check the label of any brand that you are thinking of buying. My advice would be to look for the label that shows a lady cooking with a wok.

23

Coconut Milk (ka thi)

Many people mistakenly believe that coconut milk comes from the inside of a coconut. The word 'milk' is a misnomer, as this watery substance really should be called an extract. The milk is made by grating the inner flesh of the coconut and mixing it with water. The pulp is then pressed by hand or machines to get the milk. There are two types of coconut milk: the thick one is the result of the first pressing, and the thin one comes from the second pressing. When the thicker of the two is heated, it creates fat in which pastes can be fried. Thais do not eat dairy products and rely heavily on coconut milk as a substitute.

Salty Duck Eggs (kai kem)

Duck eggs are soaked in salt water for forty days and can then be cooked in a variety of ways. They can be boiled, deep-fried, served in salads or with a sweet sauce, or made into relishes. The extraordinary flavour of the salty egg is too pungent for some, although it is an acquired taste and I would recommend persevering. These eggs are available from good Chinese and Thai grocery shops, but don't confuse them with the Chinese salty duck eggs as these black jelly eggs taste very different.

1. Pandan Leaf
2. Dried Shrimp
3. Thick Sweet Soy
4. Rice Vinegar
5. Tamarind Pulp
6. Shrimp Paste
7. Rice Vermicelli
8. Coconut Milk
9. Oyster Sauce

10. Fish Sauce
11. Red Curry Paste
12. Natural Soy
13. Palm Sugar
14. Rice Noodles
15. Dried Chillies
16. Salty Duck Eggs
17. Ming Noodles
18. Rice Paper

SPECIAL TECHNIQUES

Fish Sauce

This seasoning replaces salt, but many vegetarians will not eat fish sauce. So if you are making a vegetarian dish, you can either use salt (which will take time to cook to ensure that there is sufficient flavour) or make a brine with sea salt, preferably untreated such as sel gre from France. The quantities for the brine should be ten parts salt to four parts water. Another option would be to do what the Chinese do and substitute the fish sauce with light soy.

Crisp fried garnish

Separately, shallots, garlic,and red chillies are continually used to garnish soups, curries and rice and collectively they are used on noodle dishes.

300ml/ 1/2 pt vegetable oil

100g/3 1/2 oz Thai shallots, peeled and sliced thinly

100g/3 1/2oz garlic, peeled and sliced thinly

100g/3 1/2oz red chillies, sliced and the seeds kept in

1. Heat the oil in a pan or a wok . Add the shallots increase the heat slightly. Then fry until golden. Remove and drain.

2. Repeat the process with the garlic, followed by the chillies. Keep the oil to use later for frying or for garnishing.

Roasting Spices

Before dried spices are used they should, where possible, be roasted in a dry pan over a low heat or in a moderate oven. They will then turn slightly dark in colour and their natural oils will be released. This process intensifies the nutty flavour of the spices and helps to turn them to powder when ground. Dried chilli and dried shrimps also benefit from being roasted first.

Roasting Coconut

Take a fresh coconut and punch a small hole in the shell at one of the three eyes. This will release the water from the inside of the shell. Preheat an oven to 200°C/400°F/Gas 6 and place the coconut in the oven and roast for 30 minutes. Remove and leave to cool. Crack the shell with a hammer and remove the flesh, slicing it thinly, preferably on a mandolin. Place the strips back in the oven for 10 minutes until light brown and leave to cool. They will last about one week.

Bruising

When cooking with aromatic roots and leaves, one of the best ways to extract the flavours from them is to bruise the outer flesh and split the natural cells. This enables the natural oils to be released and the flavour to escape slowly to make an infusion. The best way to bruise is in a pestle and mortar. Gently pound the root or grass so that it splits but stays whole; if bruising leaves, then rub them in your hands and drop them into the sauce.

The Thais use many things for wrapping their food – from banana leaves to rice paper. They wrap things to protect the food during cooking to enhance the flavour or for decoration.

1. Place the filling in the centre of the wrapper and draw the two opposite ends together.
2. Fold the corners over twice to seal. The wrapper should form a cylinder.
3. Fold over each end to seal the food in.

Roasting Garlic

In Thai cookery, the garlic is first roasted in its skin. The skin is then removed and the roasted flesh used as a paste for flavouring. A whole bulb of garlic is placed in a moderate oven for 30 minutes until coloured and fragrant. It is then left to cool at room temperature and the flesh removed. Pastes and garlic are often cooked over a very high temperature, something I was guilty of before I travelled. The wok should be heated first, then the fat or coconut milk added. Before putting in the paste, the temperature should be reduced. If there is garlic to go in, it should added last. And if the garlic is in the paste, it should be cooked slowly or the garlic will burn because of its high sugar content, making the dish turn bitter.

Re-hydrating

Many dishes within the Thai repertoire require dried food to be re-hydrated. Whether it is for chillies, noodles or fish, the process remains the same. To follow the correct method, place the dried item in a bowl and cover with water, but only for a few minutes with rice vermicelli. If you want to cheat, then cover with warm to hot water but beware because even though the outer area will re-hydrate, the inside may still be dry.

Crustaceans

The cooking and preparation of crustaceans is believed to be difficult but it is, in fact, an easy process. Remember that a good quality piece of shellfish should be bought live and then placed in the freezer before being plunged into water. Placing the creatures in a freezer will send them to sleep and it is a relatively humane way of killing them. A 1kg(2¼lb) crab will take about 10 minutes to cook and a lobster about the same. When preparing a lobster, you should first split it down the centre by placing a knife between the eyes and pulling the knife down the length of the body. Then remove the tract that carries the waste from the flesh and the brown matter from under the eyes. To prepare a crab, lift off the top shell and remove the finger-like gills and the soft brown matter in the centre of the body. All the rest can be eaten. You could always get your fishmonger to show you the first time so that you can become the expert.

Frying

Deep-frying food ensures that it is sealed at a high heat and that any external bacteria are killed off instantly. Many Thai recipes also demand that food be either shallow-fried or stir-fried in large amounts of oil, sometimes as much as a cup. When the food is cooked, the excess oil is then poured away. Because of the high heat generated by the hot oil, the food seals quickly and does not absorb great quantities of oil, thereby keeping its crispness.

EQUIPMENT

28

Although to start to cook Thai food you really don't need to have any special equipment; the following two items will help to give a more authentic feel to your food.

Pestle and Mortar

There are two basic shapes. The broad based version has a large, shallow surface area to pound in and is the one that will be most useful. The pestle and mortar enables natural juices and oils to be extracted from the flesh of vegetable, meat or fish. This heightens the flavour, revealing the true essence of the food. If a food processor is used, the natural fibres are chewed and the oils are not released. This generally means that pastes and dressings go sour very quickly.

The Wok

One of the cheapest and the most useful pieces of cooking equipment that has ever been invented, the surface area allows for a large area to become hot so that the cooking process is a lot quicker than if the food was cooked in a more traditional pan. Usually made of tin, woks are light, easy to clean and they heat up very quickly. They can be put to various other uses apart from stir frying, from cooking curry, boiling noodles, deep-frying or cooking an omelette, to standing in as the base for a bamboo steamer.

Skimmer

Known in the trade as a spider. These woven pieces of wire on the end of a bamboo stick are used to take the smaller items out of the deep fryer and help to drain off the oil.

Crisp fried garnish should always be crispy and oil free. (See page 25)

Wok Spoon

A large single, metal spoon with various uses. It can be used as a measuring spoon, as a tool to move the food around the wok when frying, or as a serving spoon or tasting spoon. As these spoons have long handles, there is enough distance from the wok when cooking and the handles don't get hot.

Cleaver

In the Far East they are very good at inventing tools that have more than one function and the cleaver is a prime example. Used for thinly slicing vegetables, chopping up meat and its bones, and fish, it is also used to flatten garlic and to extract the juice from lemon grass. The cleaver is all you really need to perform most cooking tasks, along with a small knife for peeling.

31

Equipment

1. Large cleaver
2. Wok spoon with holes
3. Skimmer
4. Mandolin
5. Pestle and Mortar for Green Papaya
   Salad

6. Bamboo Steaming Basket
7. Wok Spoon
8. Small Cleaver
9. Wok
10. Pestle and Mortar

Mandolin

Available cheaply made from plastic most mandolins are imported directly from Japan. They are used for chopping vegetables and fruit and come with numerous blades which are detachable and very sharp. Please take heed of the warning on the side.

Bamboo Steamer

Bamboo steamers generally have more than one basket and can therefore sit at different levels over any pot or wok. Available in many sizes, they can take everything from a few dumplings to a whole fish. The bamboo imparts a wonderful flavour and can also be used as the serving dish.

Useful Thai Vocabulary

By learning the following words and phrases you should be able to work out what particular dishes are if they are offered to you, or written down in Thai English. All the words are pronounced phonetically. Pad prik khing, for example, is a paste of chillies with ginger. If pad prik khing moo is offered, this has the added ingredient of pork. If you see klong goong on the menu, this means freshwater river prawns. **Good luck.**

Phrik/Chilli
Phrik khi nu/Small hot chilli
Gai/Chicken
Moo/Pork
Goong/Prawn
Pla/Fish
Tom/Soup
Gaeng/Curry
Klong/River
Nuea/Beef
Sapparos/Pineapple
Nam/Sauce
Khing/Ginger
Pak Chee/Coriander
Farang/No Flavour
Nueng/Steamed
Paad/Paste

Gluay/Banana
Mamuang/Mango
Khao/Rice
Po piah/Spring roll
Som tam/Green papaya salad
Nam pla/Fish sauce with chilli
Sawadee/Welcome
Rot chart/Harmony
Krap khun krap/Thank you
Kapi/Shrimp Paste
Yaam/Salad
Yang/Grilled
Bet/Duck
Prik Thai/Peppercorns
Kai/Egg
Kai kem/Salty duck egg
Mee/Noodles

Once crabs have been boiled, crack the shells and use the meat for salads, curries, soups and noodles. And use the shells to make sauces.

1
NOODLES AND SOUPS

In Thai cooking, there are not that many classic noodle dishes. Instead, there are many variations of classics, such as Phat Thai and Chiang Mai, and several that seem to be made up by people as they go along. Noodles are always eaten as a snack and not as part of a meal. They can be bought from the many street vendors, who often make up their own special recipes. Frequently you will find a fried noodle vendor with a stand next to the soup noodle vendor. When eating on the street, it's normal to share a small plastic table with about three other people. The food is cheap and some people will eat like this a couple of times a day, sprinkling their latest purchase with huge amounts of dried chilli, and increasing the pungency by adding fish sauce.

Noodles come in many forms. For many of us, deciding which noodle to use for each dish is the hardest part. As a guideline, fresh Chinese-style oil noodles are good for frying, and rice stick and vermicelli are good for soup noodles. The classic Phat Thai uses Guay Tiaw, the broader fresh version of the dried rice noodle. These have to be soaked and cooked with hot oil, a good paste and a little water. Freshly made noodles are found in every dry land and floating market in Thailand and are left out in the sun to dry. They are then bought by the handful rather than by the weight. Where possible do try to use fresh noodles. You will find that nowadays many stores in your local Chinatown will have fresh stick noodles.

In the West, we say 'soup' and everyone thinks of the first thing you see on a restaurant menu or has visions of cold winter days. But for Thais, soup is a very different thing. Soups are eaten as a part of the meal, not at its start. They are used as a balancing agent for the other dishes and are served at the same time. This could be the reason why so many people find Thai soups far too strongly flavoured. Thai soup should be eaten with rice unless it has dumplings or noodles in it, then it becomes something quite different again.

In general, Thai soups are very quick and easy to make. It is important to use good quality, fresh ingredients in order to get the best results and flavours. Unlike Western style soups, which are cooked for long periods, the Thais have perfected the art of infusion – a process enabling the true individual flavours of various ingredients to be apparent in the finished dish. This is a very important factor to remember for anyone who starts to cook Thai: if you boil and boil a pot of Tom Yum (Thai soup), the flavours will change and the whole thing will taste soapy. A wise Thai lady with whom I once cooked told me, 'Don't boil the love out of it'.

Pumpkin cooked in spiced coconut ready to be added to the noodles.

NOODLES

Pumpkin with Noodles and Spiced Coconut

This pumpkin noodle could easily be in the curry section as it has all the makings of a curry. It uses a pad phrik or chilli paste that is fried off in coconut fat. Pumpkin is sweet and using a little lime juice helps to cut the sweetness. But having said that, it also has a great amount of spice, so go easy with the chilli paste.
Serves 8–10 as part of a meal or 4 as a main course

2 medium butternut squash or, 1kg/2lb 4oz pumpkin, peeled
350g/12oz rice noodles (sen mi)
300ml/½ pt thick coconut milk
100g/3½oz chilli paste (see page 90)
400ml/14fl oz thin coconut milk
100g/3½oz coconut cream
10 lime leaves
30g/1oz palm sugar
Thai fish sauce to taste
100g/3½oz fresh bean sprouts, picked
150g/5½oz crisp fried garnish (see page 25)
A small bunch fresh coriander, leaves picked

1. Cut, peel and de-seed squash or pumpkin. Cut into 5cm/2 inch dice.
2. Re-hydrate the rice noodles in cold water.

Pumpkin Sauce
3. Heat the thick coconut milk over a high heat until it splits and then add the chilli paste and fry for about 5 minutes, until fragrant.
4. Add the squash or pumpkin and cook for 4–5 minutes then add thin coconut milk and the coconut cream. Bring to the boil. Add the lime leaves and simmer for 20 minutes.
5. Stir in the palm sugar, and add fish sauce to taste – it should taste sweet, hot and just slightly salty.

To serve
6. Place re-hydrated noodles in a bowl, and pour the squash or pumpkin sauce over the top.
7. Garnish with bean sprouts, fried garnish and picked coriander.

Oysters and Noodles with Water Chestnuts

The Chinese influence is evident in this rather upmarket version of a Thai noodle dish, which marries classic Thai ingredients, such as lemon grass, with Chinese choy and water chestnuts. The reason it seems upmarket is because the flavourings are strained out of the soup before the other garnishes are added. When using fresh oysters, open as near to the time of use as possible, drain off the liquid through a tea strainer and add to the soup just before serving. The fresh taste of the sea water will completely transform the whole dish.
Serves 6–8 as part of a meal or 4 as a starter

Stock
1 litre/1¾ pt good chicken stock
7 pieces coriander root
5 thick slices galangal
100g/3½oz chopped ginger
5 lime leaves
3 lemon grass stalks, crushed in a mortar
1 star anise
1 cardamom pod
Fish sauce to taste
Oyster sauce

Soup
12–20 oysters, shelled
200g/7oz thick white oil noodles
100g/3½oz choi sum, shredded
4 baby corn, cut in half lengthways
100g/3½oz water chestnuts, sliced
20 snowpeas, cut on an angle
2 spring onions, sliced on an angle to garnish

1. Place all ingredients for the stock in a large saucepan and bring to the boil. Simmer for 2–3 minutes. Strain and keep stock hot on side of stove.
2. Place the oysters in the stock and cook for 30 seconds. Then add noodles, choi sum, baby corn and water chestnuts. Bring to the boil and add the snowpeas. Remove from the heat, ladle into soup bowls and garnish with spring onions.

Oysters and Noodles with Water Chestnuts

Candied Noodles

For this cold dish the noodles are fried first and then covered in a sweet and sour sticky sauce and finished with pickled garlic. When frying the noodles ensure that the oil is very
hot or they will not go crisp and fry in small batches as they expand. And give the oil a chance to recover before putting in each new load.
Serves 5–8 as part of a meal or 4 as a starter

100g/3½oz rice vermicelli
250ml/1½ pt vegetable oil
1 tbsp chopped garlic
1 tbsp chopped shallot
60g/2oz lean pork, finely chopped
60g/2oz fresh shrimp, finely chopped
1 tbsp fermented soy beans
15ml/1 tbsp white rice vinegar
15ml/1 tbsp fish sauce
60m/¼ tbsp palm sugar
1 tsp ground dried chillies
15ml/1 tbsp lime juice
1 cake yellow bean curd, cut into matchstick pieces and deep fried
2 pickled garlic bulbs, thinly sliced
11 tbsp Kaffir lime rind, finely shredded
3 stems of coriander, roughly chopped
1 chilli, thinly sliced
3 Chinese chives to garnish

1. Fry the noodles in hot oil until crisp and then drain.
2. Heat 2 tbsp of oil in a frying pan. Fry the garlic and shallots for 1–2 minutes until fragrant, then add the pork, shrimp, fermented soy beans, vinegar, fish sauce, sugar and dried chillies. Simmer for 2 minutes until thick, and add the lime juice. Adjust seasonings to obtain a sweet, sour and salty flavour.
3. Reduce the heat and continue stirring until sticky. Add the bean curd, and then spoon onto serving plates.
4. Sprinkle the pickled garlic, Kaffir lime rind, coriander, chilli and chives on top and serve.

Rice Noodles with Coconut, Pork and Prawn

In Thailand I was able to buy fresh rice noodles and vermicelli from the morning market but the dried re-constituted noodles are just as good. To get them to a flexible consistency, soak for about 60 minutes in cold water. Either add them to a sauce, or warm them in coconut milk as in this recipe.
Serves 8–10 as part of a meal or 4 as a main course

100ml/4fl oz thick coconut milk
100g/3½oz minced pork
100g/3½oz minced prawns
3 red chillies, roasted and de-seeded
30ml/2 tbsp palm sugar
2 tsp dried shrimp
30ml/2 tbsp fish sauce
500ml/18fl oz thin coconut milk
250g/1lb 2oz rice vermicelli (khamon jin)
50g/1½fl oz tofu
350g/12oz pickled turnip, chopped finely
100g/3½oz beanshoots
3 shallots, peeled and sliced
2 cloves garlic, crushed
Fresh coriander leaves
Chilli powder to taste

1. Put the thick coconut milk in a wok and cook on a high heat until it splits.
2. Add the pork and prawns with the chillies and the palm sugar and fry for 2 minutes. Add 1 tsp dried shrimp and the fish sauce.
3. Add half the thin coconut milk and bring to a simmer. Cook for 10 minutes.
4. In a separate pan, heat the remaining thin milk and add the noodles. Stir well and remove from the heat.
5. Add the tofu to the sauce. Place the noodles in bowls and cover with the sauce. Garnish with pickled turnip, remaining dried shrimp, beanshoots, sliced shallots, garlic, coriander and chilli powder.

Candied Noodles

Phat Thai

This is probably the most well known of Thai noodle dishes. As for its spelling, that depends on what part of Thailand you are in and who translates it for you! The one ingredient that is worth searching out for in this little number is the pickled turnip. Although it may not sound very appetizing, it will transform the dish.
Serves 4 as a main dish

1 bunch coriander, roots and leaves picked
100g/3½oz peeled garlic, finely chopped
500g/1lb 2oz thick dried flat rice noodles (kuai tiao)
100ml/3½fl oz vegetable oil
20 medium sized raw prawns, peeled and chopped
150g/5½oz pickled turnip, chopped
25g/1oz caster sugar
4 large eggs
4 tsp oyster sauce
50ml/2fl oz fish sauce
4 tsp lime juice
600g/1lb 5oz bean sprouts
1 bunch spring onions, trimmed and cut on the bias

100g/3½oz unsalted roasted peanuts, peeled and crushed
3 red chillies, de-seeded and finely chopped

1. Place coriander roots and garlic in a mortar and crush to form a paste. Set aside.
2. Soak the rice noodles in cold water for up to 1 hour and drain. Set aside.
3. In a wok heat the oil over a high heat. When hot and simmering, add the garlic and the coriander root paste. Stir fry for a few seconds.
4. Add the prawns and pickled turnip and cook for 30 seconds, then add the sugar. Add the egg and cook for a further 30 seconds.
5. Add the oyster sauce, fish sauce and lime juice. Add the drained noodles and cook, stirring for about 2 minutes. Add the bean sprouts and finally, finish off with the spring onions and half the crushed peanuts. Toss well.
6. Put the noodles into a serving dish and finish with picked coriander leaves, the remaining roasted peanuts and sprinkle chillies on top.
Note: if preferred, substitute the prawns with 2 thinly sliced boneless, skinless chicken breasts, or for a vegetarian version use a large finely sliced carrot and 100g/3½oz shredded bok choy.

Phat Thai

Noodles with Beanshoots and Sweet Soy

Our journey through Thailand started in Singapore so I don't want to leave out the wonderful noodles we found in the Malay street markets. For a dish with so few ingredients it is really amazing how much flavour there is, and it's the paste that is the secret of its success. Pak chee (coriander) forms a big part of this paste, and indeed of many Asian food pastes. All the flavour of coriander is in the root. Due to popular demand, it is possible to buy coriander from supermarkets with the roots intact.
Serves 4

100g/3½oz ginger root, peeled
100g/3½oz cloves garlic, peeled
30g/1oz coriander root
50ml/3 tbsp vegetable oil
1kg/2lb 4oz white thick oil noodles
100g/3½oz sugar snap peas, topped and tailed
150g/5½oz bean sprouts
100ml/3½fl oz light soy sauce
50ml/3 tbsp ketchup manis
(thick sweet soy sauce)
75ml/5 tbsp Thai fish sauce

To garnish
1 bunch of coriander (washed and the leaves picked)
200g/7oz crisp fried garnish (see page 25)

1. Pound the ginger, garlic and coriander roots to a paste in a mortar and leave to one side.
2. In a hot wok, heat the oil until shimmering. Add the ginger paste and stir fry for 1–2 minutes until fragrant.
3. Add the noodles and fry for about 2 minutes.
4. Add the sugar snaps and bean sprouts. Toss well and cook for a further minute.
5. Add the soy sauce, the ketchup manis and the fish sauce. Toss well and keep warm.
6. Pile the noodles into a serving bowl. Mix together the coriander and fried vegetable garnish and sprinkle over the top of the noodles. Serve hot.

Egg Noodles, Spring Onion and Oyster Sauce

This is a simple Chinese noodle dish which I ate a lot whilst in Singapore. The Chinatown in Singapore is fantastic, with huge areas to sit and eat food supplied by the many stallholders. They tend to concentrate on cooking only one or two things, and everything is very cheap. To me this is the best snack food.
Serves 4–6 as a side dish

6 tbsp vegetable oil
2 large eggs, beaten
500g/1lb 2oz yellow oil noodles
300g/10oz bean sprouts
4 spring onions, trimmed and chopped
½ tsp sesame oil
5g/1 tsp caster sugar
100ml/3½fl oz Thai oyster sauce
100ml/3½fl oz light soy sauce

1. Heat the wok and add the oil. Heat until smoky. Add the eggs and the noodles and stir fry for 3 - 4 minutes until warmed through.
2. Add the bean sprouts and toss well to mix. Add the spring onions and season to taste with remaining ingredients. Serve immediately.

Chiang Mai Noodle

This noodle dish from the north of Thailand uses coconut milk, which is unusual for this region. Chiang Mai noodle can be hot and has a very complex sweet flavour. Frying the noodles and putting them on top of the finished dish is very common. We ate this whilst travelling downriver by boat, on the trek. The sauce was cooked and kept hot, and the garnish prepared in advance. All we had to do was grab a bowl of noodles and cover them with the hot sauce.
Serves 4

200ml/7fl oz thick coconut milk
1 tbsp red curry paste (see page 97)
1 tbsp palm sugar

4 x 75g/2³/₄oz chicken thigh fillets, skinned
and cut into small pieces

400ml/14 fl oz thin coconut milk

1 tbsp fish sauce

200ml/7fl oz vegetable oil

750g/1lb 10oz thin egg noodles (ming)

4 Thai shallots, peeled and sliced

4 large red chillies, sliced

A handful of Thai basil leaves

5 stems coriander

1. In a wok heat the thick coconut milk until it splits and add the red curry paste. Cook for 5 minutes until fragrant.

2. Add the palm sugar and continue to cook for a further 5 minutes.

3. Stir in the chicken pieces, cook for 2–3 minutes until coloured. Add the thin coconut milk, bring to the boil and cook for 5 minutes. Season with fish sauce.

4. Heat the vegetable oil in a pan. Fry 50g/1³/₄oz of the noodles until crisp – these are for garnishing. Bring a saucepan of water to the boil and cook the remaining noodles for 2–3 minutes until tender. Drain well. Divide between four bowls. Cover each with the sauce and garnish with the shallots, red chillies, Thai basil, coriander and the fried noodles crumbled over.

Fried Noodles with Cabbage and Ginger

Ketchup manis is a thick sweet soy sauce that comes from Malaysia. It is used for all sorts of cooking and as a thick coating for many stir fries. Here it is balanced out by the fish sauce and given some punch by adding ginger. To make a vegetarian dish, leave out the fish sauce and make a strong salt water solution from 2 teaspoons boiling water and 1 teaspoon of sea salt, and use this as the seasoning or use light soy sauce.
Serves 4

1 large knob of ginger

3 cloves garlic

4 red chillies

5 coriander roots

1kg/2lb 4oz oil noodles

4 spring onions

100ml/3¹/₂ fl oz sunflower oil

100g/3¹/₂oz Chinese cabbage, sliced

100g/3¹/₂oz snake beans, cut into short lengths

100g/3¹/₂oz bean sprouts

100g/3¹/₂oz sugar snap peas, topped and tailed

2 tbsp coriander leaves

100ml/3¹/₂fl oz ketchup manis

75ml/5 tbsp Thai fish sauce

1. For the paste, peel and chop ginger and garlic. De-stalk chillies and slice across into thin rings. Finely chop the coriander roots.

2. Trim the spring onions, slice finely and reserve.

3. Pour the oil into a wok and add ginger, garlic, chilli, coriander roots, cabbage, beans, bean sprouts and sugar snap peas. Stir fry for 2–3 minutes until cooked but not overdone.

4. Add the noodles to the pan and toss to coat, then add the spring onions. Lastly, add coriander leaves and the ketchup manis and fish sauce. Mix well and serve.

SOUPS

Tom Yum with Prawns

Probably the most well known of the Thai soups, Tom Yum is exactly what Thai food is all about: an incredible punch that comes from only a few ingredients. Learning about these simple ingredients and seeing just how they work together will help you gain a really complete understanding of Thai food. The quantities in this recipe are for a mild Tom Yum, but you can make your own changes depending on your taste.
Serves 5–6 as part of a meal or 2–3 as a starter

750ml/1¼ pt light chicken stock
2 stalks lemon grass bruised and cut into 2.5cm/1 inch pieces
5 thick slices of galangal
3 coriander roots, bruised
3 lime leaves, torn
6 large prawns, shelled and de-veined
45ml/3 tbsp fish sauce
6 small green chillies, crushed
60ml/4 tbsp lime juice
A few fresh coriander leaves to garnish

1. Pour the stock into a large saucepan and bring to a rolling boil. Add the lemon grass, galangal, coriander roots and lime leaves. Simmer for 2 minutes.
2. Add the prawns, the fish sauce, chillies to taste and the lime juice. Return to the boil. Taste and adjust heat by adding more chilli if necessary. Garnish with fresh coriander leaves.

Tom Yum with Chicken

Although very similar to the Tom Yum with prawns, this recipe has less base flavour because it generally uses water, not stock. The reason for this is that if the stock is too strong, the flavour will be overpowering. The delicate flavour of this soup comes from the chicken cooking in the liquid.
Serves 6–8 as part of a meal or 4 as a starter

2 x 125g/5oz chicken breasts cut into fine strips
1 litre/1¾ pt water or light chicken stock
5 thick slices of galangal
2 large red chillies, de-seeded and cut into small pieces
6 small green chillies, crushed in a mortar
2 stalks lemon grass, bruised and cut into 2.5cm/1 inch pieces
3 coriander roots, bruised
45ml/3 tbsp fish sauce
3 lime leaves, torn
60ml/4 tbsp lime juice
10 Thai basil leaves

1. Put the chicken in a large saucepan and cover with the cold water or stock. Bring to the boil and add the galangal, red and green chillies, lemon grass and coriander roots. Simmer for 4 minutes.
2. Add the fish sauce and lime leaves. Taste and season, remove from the heat and add the lime juice and Thai basil leaves.

Tom Yum

Chicken Soup with Coconut Milk

In the south of Thailand coconuts grow in abundance and the milk extracted from their flesh is used for everything. This soup (Tom Kai Gai) should hold a lot of spice – the number of chillies indicates that – because of the natural sweetness from coconut. It is worth keeping in mind that seasoning and aromas will be used in different quantities in recipes using coconut milk than when using water or stock. It is also useful to know that if something is too overpowering, coconut can help to reduce that chilli bite at the last minute.
Serves 6–8 as part of a meal or 4 as a starter

4 stems coriander with root
2 x 125g/5oz chicken breasts sliced lengthways
1 litre/1³/₄ pt thin coconut milk
2 stalks lemon grass, cut and bruised
8 thick slices of peeled galangal
10 lime leaves, torn
4 small green chillies crushed in mortar
250ml/8fl oz thick coconut milk
60ml/4 tbsp fish sauce
60ml/4 tbsp fresh lime juice

1. Separate the coriander leaves from the stems. Crush the roots and stems, set aside.

2. Place the chicken in a large saucepan with the thin coconut milk, lemon grass, galangal and coriander stalks. Bring to the boil and simmer for 4 minutes.
3. Add the lime leaves and the chillies and stir in the thick coconut milk. Return to the boil and add the fish sauce and lime juice. Taste and correct the seasoning if necessary. Serve with the reserved coriander to garnish.

Clam and Tomato Sour Soup

It is not very often that you will see tomatoes in Thai food, as they are not native to the country. However some ingredients, including tomatoes, have been introduced into Thailand by foreign traders and often combine well with the more traditional Thai foods. You can make this soup with most shellfish and it is just as delicious when eaten with small crabs. Take care when adding the fish sauce as the salt water and the clams may make the soup salty enough.
Serves 6–8 as part of a meal or 4 as a starter

1kg/1lb 2oz clams
1 litre/1³/₄ pt lightly salted water
2 stalks lemon grass, bruised
5 thin slices galangal
2 small tomatoes, chopped
5–10 small dried chillies, roasted and broken
2–3 fresh small green chillies
15ml/1 tbsp fish sauce
5ml/1 tsp palm sugar
45ml/3 tbsp thick tamarind water
4 stems fresh coriander, roughly chopped
Crisp shallots and lime wedges to serve

1. Wash the clams and scrub clean. Pour the salted water into a large saucepan and bring to the boil. Add lemon grass, galangal and tomatoes. Bring to the boil and cook for 5 minutes.
2. Add the clams and the remaining ingredients, except the coriander. Simmer for 5 minutes or until all the clams are opened, discard the rest.
3. Taste and adjust the seasoning. Garnish with the fresh chopped coriander. Serve with crisp shallots and wedges of fresh limes.

Clam and Tomato Sour Soup

Hot and Sour Soup with Shellfish

This very extravagant soup would be served as part of a royal banquet or maybe adapted by one of the big hotel kitchens. When wealthy travellers, in the early part of the twentieth century, visited grand cities such as Bangkok and old Chiang Mai, they would arrive on the back of elephants, feast off the rich lands and waterways and would often be served a soup like this. You don't have to use all the seafood ingredients at once. Choose whatever you like best.

Serves 6–8 as a starter or 4 as part of a main meal.

1.2 litres/2 pints lightly salted water

3 stalks lemon grass, bruised and cut into 1cm/½ inch pieces

5 thick slices of galangal

225g/8oz fresh mussels

125g/4½oz fresh clams

125g/4½oz large whole prawns, shelled and de-veined

125g/4½oz baby squid, cleaned and scored so it will roll

225g/8oz firm white fish, such as monkfish, cut into 2cm/¾ inch chunks

10 lime leaves, torn

4 stalks coriander, leaves separated and roots crushed

60ml/4 tsp fish sauce

60ml/4 tbsp fresh lime juice

10 small red chillies, crushed in a mortar

A handful of Thai basil leaves

1. Pour the salted water into a large saucepan. Bring to the boil and add the lemon grass, galangal, mussels and the clams. Cook for 4–5 minutes.

2. Add the other seafood, lime leaves and the coriander roots and bring to the boil.

3. Remove from the heat and add the fish sauce and the lime juice and half the chillies. Taste and adjust the seasoning, adding more chilli if you wish or you could serve extra chilli on the side.

4. Sprinkle with the coriander and basil leaves and allow to stand for 5 minutes, to let the heat bring out their fragrance.

Spiced Soup with Grilled Prawns

It may seem a little strange at first to grill a prawn and then drop it in soup, but this is not unusual and as a hygienic measure it is very clever. When you are in a country with no refrigeration, and you're eating food such as shellfish, it is wise to ensure that the food is thoroughly cooked. There is no better way than using intense heat to destroy all surface bacteria. And it makes the food very tasty. To eat this soup properly you should chew on the shells of the prawns. It makes a great conversation piece at a party.

Serves 6–8 as a starter or 4 as a main meal

10 fresh green peppercorns

4 white peppercorns

4 pieces of coriander root

10 cloves of garlic roasted in their skin (see page 27)

450g/1lb large whole prawns

1 litre/1¾ pt lightly salted water

5 thick slices of galangal

2 stalks of lemon grass

4 dried red chillies, roasted and seeds removed

60ml/4 tbsp fish sauce

60ml/4 tbsp fresh lime juice

10 lime leaves, torn and crushed in hands

Garnish

1 handful of Thai basil

10 mint leaves

4 small red chillies crushed in a mortar

1. Make a paste from the peppercorns and coriander root in the mortar and pestle. Peel the garlic from its skin.

2. Bring the grill to a hot setting. Arrange the prawns on the grill rack and grill on each side until lightly charred. Set aside.

3. Pour the salted water into a large saucepan and bring to the boil. Add the galangal, lemon grass, garlic and the peppercorns and coriander paste. Simmer for 2 minutes and add the remaining ingredients except the garnish and return to a simmer. Remove from the heat and taste, adjust the seasoning and sprinkle the garnish over as you serve.

Coconut Soup with Crab and Herbs

This soup is as southern Thai as you can get as it uses coconut and wonderful sweet crabs. The crab is cooked in its shell – the shell is part of the seasoning, and helps make up the complex but smooth flavour to the soup. The crab must be given a fair amount of time in the oily coconut fat to seal it. Use small crabs that are laden with meat, or you can use crab claws, but the soup will not be as thick nor will the flavour be as rich.

Serves 5–6 as part of a meal or 2–3 as a starter

Flavouring

2 tsp of palm sugar, melted
50ml/2 fl oz tamarind water
45ml/3 tbsp fish sauce
5 small red chillies, crushed in a mortar

Soup

1 stalk of lemon grass
250ml/8fl oz thick coconut milk
2 x 100g/3½oz soft shell or velvet crabs, cut into 4
5 shallots, peeled and pounded in a mortar
4 lime leaves, torn and crushed in your hand
500ml/18fl oz thin coconut milk
2 cloves of garlic, roasted in their skins
Juice of 1 lime

Garnish

4 stems coriander, leaves picked
2 large red chillies, sliced

1. First make the flavouring. In a small saucepan heat the ingredients together for 2 minutes until hot but not boiling.
2. Now make the soup. Squash the thick end of the lemon grass so it looks like a spoon.
3. In a wok, heat the thick coconut milk and add the crab and pounded shallots. Cook for 5 minutes using the lemon grass as the spoon to stir.
4. Add half of the flavouring, the lime leaves and the remaining coconut milk. Bring back to the boil, stirring. Taste and adjust seasoning. Cut the lemon grass spoon into pieces and add to the soup with the roasted garlic, peeled, and the lime juice.

5. Serve with the extra flavouring on the side, and coriander and sliced chilli to garnish. Each person should have a piece of lemon grass.

Hot and Sour Soup with Mushrooms and Bean Curd

The diverse ingredients of this soup speak volumes about its origin. Buddhism is the main religion of Thailand but there are various other important cultural influences and these are reflected in many of the dishes, including this one. The ingredients also tell us that this soup has been around for a pretty long time. Altogether a classic dish in which the only protein, bean curd, is non animal.

Serves 6–8 as part of a meal or 4 as a starter

20g/¾oz dried Chinese Black mushrooms
20g/¾oz dried Wood Ear mushrooms
200g/7oz firm bean curd
A thumb sized piece fresh ginger, peeled
100g/3½oz fresh or canned bamboo shoots
60g/2oz spring onions
1 litre/1¾pt chicken stock
30g/¾oz chilli jam (see page 120)
10ml/2 tsp garlic purée
30ml/2 tbsp sweet rice vinegar
50g/1½oz mung bean sprouts to garnish

1. Soak the mushrooms in a bowl covered with warm water for 20 minutes. Drain the mushroms and cut into 3cm/1¼ inch pieces. Cut the bean curd into the same sized cubes.
2. Shred the ginger and bamboo shoots finely. Mince the spring onions in a blender or food processor.
3. Pour the stock into a large saucepan. Bring to the boil and add the minced spring onion, the chilli jam and garlic purée. Stir in the vinegar. Taste and adjust the seasoning, if necessary. Place the julienne of vegetables into bowls, pour over the soup and garnish with bean sprouts.

Clear Soup with Dumplings

In Thailand the first meal of the day is a bowl of clear soup with any left over rice added from the previous day. This is served with chillies on the side, to give it a kick. These clear soups, like Tom Yum, can be made with water and not stock; the seasoning comes from using fish sauce. The dumplings in this soup show a Chinese influence, and I am really grateful to them as dumplings are one of my favourite things. This soup would be eaten as a snack and not as part of a meal because like noodle dishes, the starch is already present, and rice is therefore unnecessary.

Serves 6–8 as part of a main meal or 4 as a starter

Soup

1 litre/1¾ pt chicken stock
1 stalk lemon grass
1 large head of ginger, peeled and sliced
3 cloves of garlic, split
1 large piece of galangal, sliced
1 small red chilli, crushed in a mortar
5 lime leaves, torn
3 star anise, broken
3 pieces of coriander root, bruised
30ml/2 tbsp fish sauce

Dumplings

1 spring onion
2 shiitake mushrooms
2 leaves Chinese cabbage
1 garlic clove, peeled
5ml/1tsp oyster sauce
5ml/1tsp soy sauce
2.5ml/½ tsp pure sesame oil
100g/3½oz pork mince
24 wonton skins
Sliced spring onion and chopped red chilli to garnish

1. Place all the ingredients for the soup in a large saucepan and bring to the boil, remove from the heat and leave to infuse on the side for 1 hour. Taste and re-season

2. For the dumplings, cut the spring onion into slivers and finely dice the mushrooms and cabbage.
3. Crush the garlic and mix with the oyster and soy sauces and add to the vegetables. Mix into the pork mince along with the sesame oil. Place in the refrigerator and leave to chill for 2 hours.
4. Take the dumpling wrappers and put a teaspoon of the pork mince in the middle. Dip your finger in water and run it around the edge of the wrapper – this will act as the seal. Fold the wrapper over to form either a triangle or a half moon – press down and seal well – if you wish, pleat the edges by pinching the dumplings together.
5. To cook, drop into boiling salted water and simmer for 4 minutes. Divide between soup bowls.
6. To serve, strain the soup to leave a clear broth, bring to the boil and pour over the hot dumplings. Garnish with spring onion and chopped chilli.

Clear Soup with Waxy Gourd

Whilst travelling, I was fortunate enough to have a number of locals cook for me. This is a dish from the Thai House (see page 140) just outside Bangkok. Waxy gourd is a vegetable that's not often used in the West but it is available from Asian food stores. It is also brilliant for bulking out a curry or similar dish. The pork and the gourd make for a very filling soup and the toasted dried shrimps are what gives the soup its glorious smoky flavour.

Serves 6–8 as part of a meal or 4 as a starter

1litre/1¾ pt water
45ml/3 tbsp fish sauce
Salt and pepper
100g/3½oz waxy gourd, peeled and chopped
100g/3½oz lean pork
15ml/1 tbsp light soy
1 clove of garlic, peeled and chopped
2 white peppercorns, crushed
1 tbsp dried shrimps, toasted
A small handful of coriander leaves to garnish

To serve

3 small red chillies, pounded

2 cloves garlic, peeled

5ml/1 tsp palm sugar

Pinch of salt

45ml/3 tbsp fish sauce

1. Pour the water into a large saucepan and bring to a simmer. Add the fish sauce, seasoning and the chopped gourd.

2. Chop the pork to a fine mince and add the soy sauce, garlic and peppercorns. Mix well and form into 12 small balls.

3. Drop into the simmering stock with the shrimps. Cook for 10 minutes. Taste and season if necessary. Garnish with the coriander leaves.

4. To serve, in a mortar and pestle pound the chillies and the garlic to a paste. Add the other ingredients and mix well. Serve this with the soup as an accompaniment.

Omelette Soup with Fresh Crab and Pea Shoots

Omelette soup is the best. It is very hot and the omelette is used as a cushion. At first use a small amount of chilli but do offer small bowls of nam phrik and dried chilli to add when eating. The pea shoots are very seasonal and are considered by the Chinese as very good luck and a sign of wealth. The word 'shoot' is a little misleading, as they are not really shoots but the fronds from the top of the young pea plant and are bright green with a small curling string. In fact they look like butterflies.

Serves 4

200ml/7fl oz vegetable oil

6 large eggs, beaten

100g/3½oz fresh crab meat

900ml/1½ pt seasoned chicken stock

75ml/½ tbsp palm sugar

15ml/1 tbsp fish sauce

50ml/2fl oz oyster sauce

15g/½oz pea shoots

10g/2 tsp chopped green shallots

1. Heat half the oil in wok until just before smoking.

2. Add half the egg and allow to bubble carefully, stirring until set and cooked through.

3. Drain off the excess oil. Add half the crab – put it into the omelette and turn over half the omelette. Cut into four with a spatula. Repeat the process using the remaining oil, egg and crab.

4. In a large saucepan, bring the stock to the boil and add the palm sugar and fish sauce.

5. In a large bowl mix the oyster sauce and the pea shoots together. Place the omelette pieces on top and pour the stock over. Sprinkle with the green shallots to serve.

Paul Blain's Spicy Soup of Smoked Fish and Coconut

Serves: 4–6

8 red shallots, charred
4 garlic cloves
600g/1lb 4oz smoked haddock
3–4 coriander roots
5ml/1 tsp roasted white peppercorns
15ml/1 tbsp vegetable oil
1ltr/1¾ pt coconut milk
30ml/2 tbsp roasted chilli jam (see page 120)
2 stems lemon grass, peeled and cleaned
4–6 sliced lengths of galangal
6 fresh Kaffir lime leaves
30–45ml/2-3 tbsp tamarind water
60ml/4 tbsp fish sauce
45–60ml/3-4 tbsp freshly squeezed lime juice
4–5 small dried red chillies, lightly roasted and coriander leaves to garnish

1. Place the red shallots and garlic cloves on the barbecue with the smoked haddock and char until coloured, tender and smoky flavoured. Remove and set aside.

2. In a pestle and mortar, pound the coriander roots and peppercorns to form a paste. Heat the vegetable oil in a wok and fry the coriander and pepper paste until fragrant. Add 250ml/8 fl oz of the coconut milk and bring to simmer. Add the roasted chilli jam, lemon grass, galangal, red shallots, garlic and lime leaves. Continue to simmer for 1–2 minutes, then add the smoked flaked fish meat and skin.

3. Simmer for 2–3 minutes allowing the flavours to infuse the coconut milk. Add the tamarind water and remaining coconut milk.

4. Season with fish sauce, remove from heat and stir in the lime juice. Serve immediately, garnished with the roasted small chillies and some fresh coriander leaves.

2
SNACKS AND SALADS

We are all nibblers at heart. This is the real reason, I believe, that Thai food has become so popular. When a huge plate of Thai fish cakes and prawn rolls is passed around, few people will refuse, and once you have had one then there is no going back! This also how Thais seem to spend their days. The street markets are always open and the good ones have queues. I have fond memories of lining up behind the office workers at 11 a.m. for the first fish cakes of the day having only just eaten two sticks of satay from the vendor around the corner. I then moved on about ten paces to the lady who made sweet pancakes wrapped in newspaper, with a filling of duck egg, condensed milk and sugar.

In Thailand it is in the evening when the real socializing takes place. Vendors are not only on the streets, but also on the klongs where they float up and down, selling their wares. Nearly everything comes in clear plastic bags secured by a rubber band. On some stalls you will get a bag of fish cakes, on others a bag filled with sweet chilli sauce and others a bag containing a sliced-up cucumber. You can then go and buy a soft drink that will be decanted into another bag with a straw sticking out of it.

One of the problems with this sort of snack food is that it is fiddly, taking time and patience to prepare. But it is worth persisting as the food is truly wonderful. Real addicts might just decide to fly to Thailand instead. We usually keep our salads for the summer, so imagine being able to eat a salad at any time of the year because the climate allows it. Salads conjure up visions of crisp lettuce and of tomato juice dribbling down the chin. But in Thailand salads are different – full of real 'smack in the mouth' flavour. The base of the salad can be anything from sour, unripe green papaya and mango to noodles, to slow braised meat.

Salads, like soups, are part of the main meal and contribute to the overall balance of flavours on the table. As with all Thai food the basic flavours – sweet, sour, salty and hot – should be carefully balanced. Learning to appreciate the flavour of each individual ingredient and the best combinations takes time, but then that is what cooking is all about!

If refrigeration hadn't been invented we would be still shopping every day as they do throughout Thailand. Ingredients used in Thai salads must be very fresh. Thai people have the advantage of markets that offer food most often picked in the late evening when the sun is disappearing. It is then driven to market and sold before the sun rises. Without this freshness the salad ingredients would not be able to stand up to the intensity of the different dressings which give them their power and life.

Thai Fish Cakes

SNACKS

Thai Fish Cakes with Cucumber and Sweet Chilli Sauce

This is one of the easiest Thai snacks, but it is also one of the most misunderstood. The texture of the fish cake should be slightly rubbery with a tough outer coating. They should contain a good amount of spice and lots of lime leaves. To achieve a texture similar to the fish cakes from street stalls you should literally throw the paste into a bowl several times to make the mixture more elastic.
Makes about 20

100g/3½oz skinless salmon fillet
100g/3½oz skinless cod fillet
150g/5½oz prepared squid or cuttlefish
30g/1¼oz red chilli paste
4 lime leaves, shredded
2 snake beans, chopped
30g red chilli paste
15ml/1 tbsp fish sauce
1 large egg white
15ml/1 tbsp Thai oyster sauce
Oil for deep frying

Chilli Sauce
25ml/5 tbsp white rice vinegar
75g/2¾oz granulated sugar
3 long red chillies

Garnish
20g/¾oz diced red chilli
20g/¾oz diced cucumber
15g/½oz chopped roasted peanuts

1. Blend in a food processor, the salmon, cod and squid or cuttlefish until smooth. Add the chilli paste and pulse until well mixed.
2. Place all the other ingredients, except the oil, in Mix all together and knead for 5 minutes until smooth and elastic.
3. Shape into small flat discs about 5cm/2 in wide. Heat oil for deep frying in a wok and deep fry for 4 minutes until golden. Drain on kitchen paper.

4. For the chilli sauce, place the vinegar, sugar and whole chillies in a small saucepan and bring to the boil. Simmer for 15 minutes and remove from the heat. Place in a food processor and blend until smooth. Strain and leave to cool, then add the diced chilli.
5. Serve with fish cakes, and garnish with cucumber and peanuts.

Minced Chicken in Pandan

Chicken in pandan is cooked mainly in restaurants rather than on the streets and is usually made with cubes of chicken soaked in red vinegar and soy. A Thai lady showed me this recipe using chicken mince. The pandan leaf imparts a smoky flavour when deep fried. Don't attempt to eat the leaves: they are only there as a wrapper and to add to the flavour.
Makes 12

100g/10½ oz boneless chicken, minced with skin
20ml/4tsp Thai oyster sauce
15ml/1 tbsp black bean sauce
1 spring onion, chopped
2 cloves garlic, peeled and deep fried
12 pandan leaves
Vegetable oil for deep frying

1. In a bowl, mix together all the ingredients except the pandan leaves and oil.
2. Clean and flatten the pandan leaves. Divide the mince into 12 and roll into balls.
3. Hold a pandan leaf with the pointed end to the sky and place the chicken 4cm/1½in from the base then fold the end of the leaf up over the chicken. Twist the remaining leaf around the chicken so as to cover all the meat. Push the pointed tip under the first layer and pull tight to secure the parcel.
4. Heat the oil for deep frying in a wok. Bunch the pandan leaves by holding them by the pointed end, when the oil is hot enough to deep fry. Lower the parcels into the oil, fry for 7–8 minutes until cooked through. Serve immediately.

Minced Chicken in Pandan

Satay

In the main vegetable market in Bangkok, Pak Klong Talat, I had satay for breakfast on more than one occasion. Even without the sauce they are a must, and are so addictive you have to buy them in multiples. A couple of tips when making satay: soak the sticks in warm water for 1 hour before you start. This will prevent the stick from splintering and also avoid it burning when placed on the barbecue or in the frying pan. Try to leave the meat to marinate for 24 hours to tenderize as it makes it easier to thread. Don't be tempted to grill satay because grilling will dry out the meat.
Makes about 20

400g/14oz lean beef, pork or boneless chicken, cut into thin 4cm/1½in long strips
15ml/1 tbsp light soy sauce
15ml/1 tbsp sesame oil
12 bamboo skewers
25ml/5 tsp coconut cream
1 tbsp red curry paste (see page 97)
15ml/1 tsp fish sauce
15ml/1 tbsp palm sugar
60ml/4 tbsp tamarind water
150g/5½oz roasted peanuts, chopped
100ml/3½oz thin coconut milk

1. Place the meat in a shallow bowl and mix in light soy sauce and sesame oil. Cover and chill for 24 hours. Soak the skewers in warm water for 1 hour. Thread meat on to skewers and chill until required.
2. In a saucepan, combine coconut cream and red curry paste. Bring to the boil and simmer for 5 minutes. Add the fish sauce, palm sugar, tamarind water and chopped peanuts. Cook for a further 5 minutes. Add thin coconut milk .
3. Cook each skewer over hot coals or on a griddle plate or a heavy frying pan for 1 minute on each side. Serve with the sauce, hot or cold.

Minced Chicken on Lemon Grass

This is one of those recipes that Thais disagree about. It is said that the 'real' recipe called for the chicken to be wrapped around sugar cane rather than lemon grass. The sugar cane would give a caramel sweetness to the flavour of the chicken. Whichever way you do it, it tastes great. If you are using the lemon grass, make sure that the stalks are well bruised to release all the flavour.
Makes 10

12 stalks lemon grass
4 coriander roots, chopped
7 white peppercorns, crushed
2 Thai shallots, sliced very finely
10ml/2 tsp fish sauce
1 large egg white
1 lime leaf, shredded
300g/10½oz minced chicken
Oil for deep frying

1. Trim the lemon grass on both ends to create a stick about the same length as a pencil. Remove the husk and peel by about four layers. Soak in water for approximately 10 minutes. Pound the coriander roots and peppercorns together in a mortar to form a paste.
2. Mix all the other ingredients except the oil together in a large bowl until completely mixed. Break the mixture up into 12 pieces and shape around the end of each lemon grass stalk.
3. Heat the oil in a wok and deep fry for approximately 5–6 minutes until golden and cooked through.

61

Vegetarian Spring Rolls with Sweet Chilli and Peanuts

In Thailand food is made spicy by using chilli or peppercorns. To give these spring rolls a little bite, use peppercorns in the paste, making sure that they are crushed well. This paste will provide the backdrop for the other flavours that go into these spring rolls. You should make sure that you fry them thoroughly. Meat and fish can be used instead of tofu for the base, but any meat used should be lean.
Makes 25 large or 50 small

200g/7oz rice vermicelli (khamon jin)
20 whole white peppercorns
2 cloves garlic, peeled
1 small knuckle root ginger, peeled
10 stalks fresh coriander, roots and leaves separated
Vegetable oil for deep frying
100g/3½oz minced tofu
100g/3½oz carrots, finely shredded
50g/1¾oz palm sugar
30ml/2tbsp light soy sauce
100g/3½oz bean sprouts
3 Thai shallots, peeled and sliced
50g/1¾oz plain flour
100g/3½oz red cabbage, finely shredded
25 large spring roll wrappers

1. Soak the noodles in warm water for about 10 minutes, then drain and cut into 2cm/¾in pieces.
2. Make a paste by pounding the peppercorns, garlic, ginger and coriander root in a mortar. Heat a little of the oil in a wok and fry for 3 minutes. Add the tofu, carrots and the palm sugar and cook for a further 3 minutes.
3. In a large bowl place the noodles and pour the hot mix over the top – the noodles will absorb the excess liquid and re-hydrate. Allow to cool.
4. Add the soy sauce and adjust the seasoning. Add the remaining ingredients (except the oil and the wrappers) and mix well. Cover and chill for 2 hours.
5. Separate the spring roll wrappers and place them under a damp cloth to prevent drying out. One at a time, lay a wrapper on the work surface in front of you in the shape of a diamond. Place a good tablespoonful of mixture a quarter of the way up the wrapper. Fold the end over, tuck it under and pull back so it is tight. Continue to roll up and pull back until three quarters of the way up the wrapper.

Then fold the sides into the centre. If there is sufficient mixture the two side points will meet.

6. Continue to roll to leave the tip exposed. Brush the tip with a mixture of cold water and flour, roll over and leave to set.

7. Heat the remaining oil in a wok and deep fry four rous at a time for 6–7 minutes until golden and crisp. Drain well and serve immediately.

Deep fried Stuffed Chillies

If there is a devil, this is what he must have for lunch. Although the recipe sounds ferocious, it is not that bad as long as all the membrane has been removed from the chillies prior to the stuffing process. In winter in the northern hemisphere, large green and yellow chillies can be found in some shops and these are better if you like the idea of this recipe, but can't take too much spice and heat.
Makes 12

12 mild green fresh chillies
125g/4½oz lean ground minced pork
3 tbsp crushed roast peanuts
2 tsp fish sauce
1 clove garlic, crushed
2 tsp finely chopped coriander
1 small egg
Salt and pepper
60g/2oz plain flour and extra for dusting
Oil for deep frying
3 large eggs

1. Take a knife and slit along one side of the chillies. Scrape out seeds carefully without splitting the chilli. Blanch in boiling water for a few seconds. Drain.

2. Mix the pork with the peanuts, fish sauce, garlic, coriander and small egg. Season with salt if needed. Use a teaspoon to stuff the chillies with the pork mixture. Smooth off the filling.

3. Mix the flour with enough ice water to make a thin batter. Lightly coat the stuffed chillies with a little more flour and then coat with batter. Heat the oil for deep frying in a wok and fry in hot oil for 3 minutes or till cooked, turning 3-4 times until crisp and golden. Drain on paper.

4. Beat 3 large eggs well. Strain one third of the egg into a small funnel. Hold your finger over the end and drizzle into the fryer moving across to form a thin stream. Turn the mix over. Lift out and drain on paper. Cook the remaining egg mixture in the same way.

5. Divide egg mix and wrap around chillies. Serve at once. Serve with a dipping sauce.

Chinese Fried Dumplings

Strictly speaking, these dumplings shouldn't be in a book about Thai food, but my love for dumplings and the fact that this was given to me by a street vendor, has meant they make an appearance. Once made they can be frozen. They can also be cooked from frozen – don't allow them to defrost as they will go all soggy. Eat with soy sauce and fresh chopped small chillies.
Serves 50

200g/7oz minced pork
30g/1oz chopped spring onion
15ml/1 tbsp vegetable oil
30g/1oz coriander root, pounded in a mortar
15g/½oz chopped garlic
3 fresh chillies, chopped
Fish sauce to taste
50 large wonton wrappers
1 small egg, beaten
Oil for deep frying

1. Mix together the pork and the spring onion. In a wok heat 1 tablespoon of oil and fry the coriander root and the garlic for 1 minute. Then add the pork mix and cook for a further 2 minutes and leave to cool. Add the chilli and fish sauce to taste. Leave to cool.

2. Place wonton wrappers on table. Put some of the minced pork in centre and brush around the edge of each wrapper with egg to seal.

3. Fold wonton corner to corner so triangle is formed. Place on tray until required.

4. Heat the oil for deep frying and deep fry the dumplings for 5-6 minutes until golden. Drain and serve.

63

SALADS

Green Papaya Salad with Salty Duck Egg

Enjoying the wonderful flavour of any papaya salad is one thing, but eating it with a deep-fried salty duck egg is another. The extraordinary flavour of the salty duck egg is too pungent for some people; it seems it is a bit of an acquired taste. Salty duck eggs take up to 4 weeks to make at home but they are also available from good Chinese and Thai grocery shops. Don't confuse them with Chinese salty ducks that are black and not the same at all. *Serves 8–10*

Papaya Salad

500g/1lb 2oz green papaya
250g/9oz green mango
25g/1oz peeled sliced Thai shallots
15g/½oz dried shrimps, roasted
½ bunch coriander

Dressing

6 cloves garlic, peeled
4 shallots, peeled
4 coriander roots
10 green chillies, de-seed 8 of them
½ stalk lemon grass
100g/3½oz palm sugar
100ml/3¼floz lime juice
2 tbsp fish sauce
Fresh coriander and Thai basil to garnish

Salty Duck Eggs

300g/10½oz salt
10 duck eggs
Oil for deep frying

1. Peel the green papaya and green mango and slice both very finely on a mandolin. Set aside.
2. Slice the shallots very finely and pound the dried shrimps in a mortar and pestle to a powder. Mix with the shallots.
3. Mix the shallots, coriander and the papaya mixture together and leave to one side.
4. For the dressing, in a mortar and pestle crush the garlic, shallots, coriander roots, chillies and lemon grass to a paste. Add the sugar and crush again to a paste. Add the lime juice and fish sauce and taste.
5. Bring 700ml/1¼pt water to the boil and add the salt. Stir well to make sure that it has dissolved. Remove from the heat and allow to cool.
6. Lay the eggs in a preserving jar or plastic container with a lid. Pour the cold liquid over the eggs. Seal well and date. Store in a cool, dry place for a minimum of 4 weeks.
7. To cook the eggs, bring a saucepan of water to the boil, gently lower in the eggs and boil for 7 minutes. Remove from the heat and refresh in cold water.
8. Heat oil for deep frying in a wok to 200°C/400°F and deep fry until crisp. Cut into three pieces.
9. To serve, pour the dressing mixture over the green papaya mixture and leave to one side for one hour. Place the pickled green papaya salad on a plate. Top with the deep fried hot egg and add some more dressing. Sprinkle with fresh coriander and Thai basil and serve.

Green Papaya Salad with Salty Duck Egg

Glass Noodle and Herb Salad

Glass Noodle and Herb Salad

Glass noodles are usually made from mung beans and therefore are called mung bean thread. They are sometimes used in soups and similar dishes but they should never be fried. To re-hydrate the noodles, just cover with cold water and leave until tender.
Serves 8–10

300g/10½oz glass noodles (khanom jin) re-hydrated
Juice of 3 limes
1 clove garlic, finely chopped
2 Thai shallots, finely chopped
2 long red chillies, finely chopped
40g/1½oz palm sugar
40ml/8 tsp fish sauce
30g/1oz coriander root, bruised in a mortar
1 tbsp sunflower oil
2 Thai shallots, finely sliced
1 clove garlic, finely sliced
15g/½oz Vietnamese mint
15g/½oz round mint
15g/½oz Thai basil
10 leaves pak chee laos
1 cucumber, shredded

1. Make a nam Jim by pounding the lime juice, chopped garlic and shallots, red chillies, palm sugar, fish sauce and coriander root together.
2. Heat the oil in a wok and fry the sliced shallots and garlic for 1 minute until golden. Drain well.
3. Pick all herbs (remove the leaves) and mix with the cucumber.
4. To serve, combine herbs, noodles and nam Jim.

Pork Larp

If one dish will convert you to Thai food, it is this one. With any amount of chilli it has that beautiful classic Thai flavouring: sweet, sour, salty and hot. The authentic larp is made with offal, such as liver and lung. All the meat is chopped up, not minced (as it is here for ease), and the meat remains uncooked (in this recipe it is cooked!). The meat is cured using fish sauce and lime juice. Whilst travelling in Thailand a local lady made me a larp of chicken, which was equally delicious. A word of warning, beware the roast chilli powder – it is very hot. Oh, and watch out for the dust…
Serves 4

400g/14oz finely minced pork
30ml/2 tbsp fish sauce
90ml/6 tbsp lime juice
8 red shallots, sliced
60ml/4 tbsp fresh mint, torn
60ml/4 tbsp fresh coriander, torn
60ml/4 tbsp roast sticky rice
30ml/2 tbsp roast chilli powder
2 large red chillies, de-seeded and finely shredded
15g/½oz picked coriander

1. Simmer the pork in a small saucepan with a little salted water for 3 minutes or until cooked. Remove from the heat and allow to cool.
2. Just before serving, add fish sauce, lime juice and rest of the ingredients, except the chillies and coriander. Check that flavour is salty and sour. Add a few extra drops of lime juice to adjust the seasoning if necessary.
3. Garnish with chillies and picked coriander.

69

Grilled Quail Salad

Both small and large birds are placed over hot coals in many parts of northern and southern Thailand. The open coals impart the smokiness that adds that little bit extra to Thai street food. It never tastes quite so good out of a pan, so save this one up for the summer when the barbecue is lit and you are in the mood for something a little bit different.
Serves 4

4 quail, de-boned
100g/3 1/2oz rice vermicelli, soaked (khanom jin)
2 large red chillies, finely shredded
100g/3 1/2oz snake beans, blanched and cut
4 lime leaves, finely shredded
A handful Thai basil, picked
A handful coriander, picked
4 Thai shallots, sliced
50g/1 3/4oz galangal, finely shredded

Dressing
2 small red chillies
100ml/3 1/2fl oz fish sauce
100ml/3 1/2fl oz lime juice
50g/1 1/3oz palm sugar

1. Skewer each quail using 2 skewers per bird from leg to wing on the diagonal, so that the skewers cross in the middle. Grill the quail over hot coals or on a griddle plate for 3–4 minutes on each side until cooked but slightly pink.
2. Pound the dressing ingredients together in the mortar and pestle.
3. Mix all salad ingredients in a bowl together.
4. To serve, pile salad on to serving platter and top with grilled quail.

Squid Salad with Green Mango

The green mango is sometimes seen as the poor cousin of the green papaya. It does, however, keep its crunch and adds a third dimension to a salad. These little beauties are all flesh as they are picked so young – before the seed has had the chance to form. There is a great difference between the Indian green mango and the Thai variety; the Indian is very small and slightly powdery.
Serves 4

4 tbsp corn oil
500g/1lb 2oz prepared squid
2 small firm green mangoes, peeled and finely shredded
4 Thai red shallots, sliced
20g/3/4oz fresh coriander leaves
15g/1/2oz fresh mint leaves
50g/1 3/4oz roasted peanuts, crushed

Dressing
5 small green chillies
30g/1oz palm sugar
150ml/1/4 pt fish sauce
5 tbsp lime juice
150g/5 1/2oz crisp fried garnish (see page 25)

1. Heat the oil in a wok until hot. Fry the squid very quickly for 1–2 minutes. Remove, drain and allow to cool.
2. Combine the squid with the mangoes, sliced shallots, coriander, mint and peanuts.
3. Pound all the dressing ingredients together in a mortar and pestle and toss into the squid mixture.
4. Sprinkle the deep-fried garnish over the top and serve with extra dressing.

Green Papaya Salad

This most famous of Thai salads is sold on the streets in Bangkok. Each of the street vendors must have the stamina of an ox, as they spend the best part of their day pounding the ingredients for this salad. It is always made fresh and in front of you and you can make any request for extras that you want. The real big boys and girls eat theirs with extra chilli powder, but I find that the best way to cope with the heat is to go for sticky rice, which acts as a buffer. For novices, I would suggest using half the quantity of chillies in the recipe. And remember, the fresher the lime juice, the bigger the zing.
Serves 6

70

5 green small green chillies
3 cloves garlic
1 tbsp chopped palm sugar
300g/10½oz unripe green papaya (peeled and cut en julienne)
1 tbsp fish sauce
1 tbsp dried shrimps
6 cherry tomatoes (quartered)
50g/1¾oz snake beans, cut into 1cm (1½ in) lengths
3 tbsp lime juice
2 tbsp unsalted roasted peanuts

In a large ceramic mortar and pestle pound the chillies, garlic and palm sugar. Add the papaya and pound again then add the fish sauce and the shrimps; pound again. With a large spoon stir in the tomatoes, snake beans and the lime juice. Garnish with the peanuts.

Braised Beef Salad with Roast Rice

It is well known that Thais will make sure that no food is wasted and whatever they eat must be very fresh. Without the benefit of refrigeration, beef must be killed and eaten within a few days or it has to be cured. By using fish sauce as the curing agent, the life of the meat is prolonged. It also acts as a tenderizer and enhances the flavour. The best result seems to be achieved by using meat with large amounts of sinew, which then gets broken down in the process and prevents the meat from drying out. The fat in the coconut milk, along with the lemon grass, galangal and lime leaves, provides the flavour. The worst part of this recipe is washing up the tray that you cook the beef in.
Serves 4

Braised Beef
400g/14oz sirloin beef trimmings
100ml/3½fl oz fish sauce
300ml/½ pt canned coconut milk, shaken well
1 large piece galangal, peeled and chopped roughly
1 stalk lemon grass, bruised

10 lime leaves

Dressing
4 dried red chillies
100ml/3½fl oz lime juice
30ml/2 tbsp fish sauce
1tbsp/15ml palm sugar

Salad
100g/3½oz shredded green mango
50g/1¾oz lemon grass, thinly sliced
50g/1¾oz Thai shallots, peeled and thinly sliced
15g/½oz coriander leaves
A few mint leaves
A few Thai basil leaves, torn
15g/½oz roast rice

1. Place the beef trimmings in a large bowl and cover with the fish sauce. Cover and chill for 24 hours.
2. Next day drain the beef from fish sauce and put in large roasting tray with coconut milk, galangal, lemon grass and lime leaves.
3. Bake in a pre-heated oven at 190°C/375°F/Gas 5 for 40 minutes. Turn the beef over and increase heat to 200°C/400°F/Gas 6. Cook for a further 40 minutes, checking at least once to see how it is going.
4. After the further 40 minutes turn up temperature to 240°C/475°F/Gas 9 and bake for 10 minutes until golden and most of the milk has evaporated.
5. Remove from oven and leave. Shred the beef. Set aside ready to be mixed through the salad.
6. For the dressing, preheat the oven to 180°C/250°F/Gas 4. Remove seeds from the dried chillies and roast on a baking tray for 10 minutes until black. Allow to cool.
7. Pound chillies then add fresh lime juice, fish sauce and palm sugar – it should be a hot and sour tasting sauce, be careful of adding salt.
8. When making the salad – put all the ingredients except the dressing and rice in the bowl. Add the beef and mix well. Spoon over the dressing just before serving and garnish with roast rice.

71

Crisp Taro Salad with Crabmeat

The vegetable, taro, is not widely used. The Chinese use it for its thickening properties in soups and porridge. When first sliced, the best taro ooze with a thick sticky white sap, whereas the older woodier ones will not. As the slices deep fry they change to a mottled brown colour and have a slight peppery aftertaste. They make a great alternative to potato crisps, and salt will enhance the flavour. Like a packet of crisps they're not easy to stop eating.
Serves 4–6

Dressing

100ml/3½fl oz fresh lime juice
100ml/3½fl oz coconut vinegar
20ml/4 tsp fish sauce
20ml/4 tsp caster sugar

Salad

400g/14oz freshly cooked crabmeat
3 spring onions, finely chopped into rounds
1 large red chilli, finely diced
1 tbsp pickled ginger, finely diced
1 heaped tbsp mint leaves, cut en julienne
1 tbsp chopped coriander
½ cucumber, cut en julienne
50g/1¾oz sliced Thai shallots
2 lime leaves, cut very fine en julienne
5 tomatoes, finely diced
Salt and pepper
400g/14oz medium sized taro root, thinly sliced and deep fried
Assorted lettuces leaves

1. First make the dressing by combining all the ingredients together.
2. In a bowl mix the crabmeat, spring onions, chilli, diced pickled ginger, chopped herbs, cucumber, Thai shallots, lime leaves and diced tomatoes. Season lightly.
3. Pour over half the dressing and allow to stand for 2 minutes.
4. Arrange the crabmeat between the taro root crisps, place in the centre of the plate and arrange the salad leaves around. Drizzle around the remaining dressing and serve.

Note: To deep fry taro root, heat oil for deep frying in a wok to 220°C/450°F and fry the taro for 2–3 minutes, turning, until golden.

Grilled Chicken Salad with Cucumber and Coconut

There has always been controversy over whether to use chicken thighs in this recipe rather than breast meat. As with any meat on the barbecue, it needs fat to help it keep moist. Chicken breast meat without the skin will dry out in no time. The meat is steeped in coconut milk that gives the outer flesh a caramel crisp surface with a buttery inner layer of cooked coconut cream. Chillies are optional.
Serves 4–6

400g/14oz boneless chicken thighs
100ml/3½fl oz thick coconut milk
40g/1½oz palm sugar
50ml/2fl oz fish sauce
2 bunches coriander, picked
50g/1¾oz red chilli, sliced
1 cucumber, sliced
50g/1¾oz Thai shallots, finely sliced
50g/1¾oz roasted peanuts, crushed
50g/1¾oz roasted coconut

1. Place the chicken in a shallow dish. Pour over the coconut milk. Cover and chill for 2 hours. Drain chicken, reserving coconut, and place on barbecue or griddle plate. Cook for 5 minutes on each side, then transfer to the oven to cook for a further 10 minutes. Allow to cool then slice up as thinly as possible, about ½cm (¼in) thick.
2. Pour reserved coconut milk into a saucepan and bring to boil, season with palm sugar and fish sauce – it should be salty before sweet. Remove from the heat and allow to cool.
3. Assemble the salad with the chicken, coriander leaves, sliced chilli, sliced cucumber, Thai shallots and roasted peanuts. Toss together and then add the cooked coconut dressing to serve, with remaining dressing and garnished with roasted coconut.

Grilled Chicken Salad with Cucumber and Coconut

3
STEAMED AND FRIED

One single chapter dedicated to steaming and frying in a book about Thai food may, in a way, seem a little inadequate. However, many of the steamed and fried dishes in this section use basic principles which will allow you to mix and match with other dishes with ease.

Steaming is a very quick way to cook food properly while preserving the natural flavours and textures. It is a particularly appropriate method of cooking delicate foods and is the ideal way to cook fish whole. It is also good for cooking small morsels such as scallops quickly, before they take on the flavour of a sauce, such as hot peanut oil. Remember that steaming is a far more penetrating method than boiling – a whole bass can take as little as twelve minutes to cook.

It is worth investing in a large bamboo steamer (if you can, get one in Thailand, as the flavours it gives off are amazing) but if not, use a metal steamer or just place a colander over boiling water. Do make sure that the water does not get inside whatever you are using. Always line your steamer with greaseproof paper or with a fragrant banana leaf – this will prevent the steamer marking the food. Fill your wok with water up to the base of the bamboo steamer. Bring the water to the boil. Have the food in the steamer ready and place it over the water, taking care that you don't get burnt by the steam.

Frying is defined as 'the application of heat to food with the assistance of oils or fat' and is often used in Thai cooking. However, contrary to popular belief, most foods are fried in a lot of fat. There is still a great difference between deep frying and stir frying, but when you stir fry and you don't use enough fat, your food will braise or stew, destroying the texture and fresh flavour of the food.
Don't be afraid to use lots of fat when you stir fry and pour off the excess before you serve your meal.

Before the mass production of vegetable oil, Thais would have used rendered animal fat and the oil gained from splitting coconut milk. Using coconut oil or animal fat will make a big difference to the flavour of your finished dish. It's worth looking out for coconut oil in Chinese shops, before taking the easy option and reaching for the vegetable oil.

Steamed Scallops

Cod Steamed with Lime in Banana Leaf

The wonderful flavours given off by leaves when you cook with them are sometimes hard for Westerners to appreciate. Thais use leaves all the time, whether it be for steaming or roasting but we never use the leaf as an outer layer to cook things in. Wrapping the fish in this recipe in banana leaf and steaming it imparts a lovely nutty flavour to the fish.
Serves 4

200g/7oz root ginger, peeled
2 large banana leaves
300g/10½oz cooked sticky coconut rice
4 x 200g/7oz pieces of cod fillet
50ml/2fl oz fish sauce
4 tsp ground white peppercorns
2 limes, rind removed and julienned

1. Thinly slice half the ginger and finely shred the other half. Cut the banana leaves into 10 x A4 size pieces.
2. Bring a large saucepan of water to the boil and blanch banana leaf squares for 2–3 minutes. Drain well.
3. Place a layer of rice on each leaf and lay sliced ginger over it. Place fish on top.
4. Season fish with fish sauce, white pepper, lime rind and julienne of ginger.
5. Wrap the banana leaf around the fish. Steam for 20 minutes until tender and serve.

Steamed Scallops

Scallops are simply one of the most delicious morsels pulled from our seas and they deserve great respect. They must be cooked very quickly and over a high heat to stop them shrinking and turning into bullets. Only the soft inner section of the lemon grass can be eaten, so the outer two or three layers need to be removed. Keep the outer layers though and use them to make lemon grass tea, which you can drink with the meal.
Serves 6

2 stalks lemon grass
4 Thai shallots
2 large red chillies
2 small green chillies
1 tsp palm sugar
1 tsp fish sauce
Juice of 2 limes
24 shelled scallops
A handful coriander leaves
A handful mint leaves
3 tbsp peanut oil

1. Remove the outer layer of the lemon grass and reserve for making tea if liked. Slice very finely. Peel and slice the Thai shallots. De-seed the red chillies and slice into thin strips.
2. Make a dressing by crushing the green chillies with the palm sugar together in a pestle and mortar. Add the fish sauce and the fresh lime juice at the end.
3 Bring a saucepan or wok of water to the boil. Place the scallops inside a steamer and cook over the boiling water for 3–4 minutes so they are just cooked but have not shrunk.
4. Mix together the coriander, mint and the prepared shallot and red chilli. Divide between 6 plates and sprinkle with some of the dressing.
5. Heat the oil in a small saucepan until hot.
6. Divide the scallops between the plates and place the sliced lemon grass on top. Now pour the boiling oil on to the lemon grass to release the flavour. Serve immediately.

Whole Steamed Bream and Ginger

Steaming a whole fish can be the most
economical way of cooking it. Steam ensures
that all the natural juices stay within the fish
and that shrinkage is minimal. When you buy
a fish for steaming choose a whole fish with the
guts and head still intact. Ask the fishmonger
to remove the guts through the gills without
slitting the belly open. This will help the fish
stay together when it is being steamed and
stops any part of the fish overcooking.
Serves 2

800g/1lb 12oz whole sea bream, snapper
or talapia, gutted and scaled

75ml/5 tbsp Shao shing wine

30g/1oz caster sugar

4 tsp sesame oil

150ml/¼ pt light soy sauce

15g/½oz fresh ginger cut en julienne

4 tsp peanut oil

15g/½oz sliced spring onion

15g/½oz coriander leaves

1. Score each side of the fish in a criss-cross
pattern through to the bone, place on a plate.
Mix together the wine, sugar, sesame oil and soy
sauce and pour over the fish. Sprinkle over the
ginger.
2. Transfer the plate with the fish on to a
steamer. Cover and steam until flesh is firm
(7–10 minutes). Remove from steamer and
place on a serving platter.
3. Heat the oil in a small saucepan until
smoking hot.
4. Sprinkle the fish with sliced spring onion and
coriander leaves and pour smoking hot peanut
oil over fish. Serve with steamed rice.
Note: Ask your fishmonger to prepare the fish
for you.

Steamed Egg with Pork and Prawn

People have been steaming eggs in a custard for a long time, each nation and every subsequent generation adding its own flavourings. Italians add cheese, and the Japanese make a savoury custard with prawns and serve it with pickled ginger. The secret of a successful steamed egg dish is to remove it from the steamer when the centre is still slightly wobbly. If it cooks all the way through it will be overcooked by the time it gets eaten.
Serves 6

6 large eggs
60ml/4 tbsp light soy sauce
500ml/18fl oz chicken stock
3 white peppercorns, crushed
50g/1¾oz pork mince
1 tsp fish sauce
6 large prawns, peeled and chopped
2 Thai shallots, peeled and sliced
3 spring onions, trimmed and chopped

Garnish

2 lime leaves, thinly sliced
A few coriander leaves
2 large red chillies, cut on an angle with seeds

1. In a large bowl stir together the eggs, soy, stock and pepper.
2. In another bowl, mix together the pork mince with the fish sauce, prawn, shallots, and spring onions. Add half the mince to the egg mixture and pour into 6 heatproof ramekin or small baking dishes.
3. Bring a saucepan or wok of water to the boil. Place the dishes in a steamer over the water. Sprinkle the remaining pork mixture over the top of each dish and place a lid on the steamer. Cook for 10–12 minutes until just set.
4. Remove from the steamer and garnish with the lime leaves, coriander and chopped chillies.

Steamed and Fried Squid filled with Pork

It is not unusual for a Thai dish to require two if not three different cooking methods. By steaming the filled squid in this recipe, the filling will be cooked through and the squid exterior will be tenderized. The final process of frying will produce a crisp outer and very tender inside. Thais use this process often. They are very ingenious cooks.
Serves 4

12 white peppercorns
3 cloves garlic
6 pieces coriander root
200ml/7fl oz vegetable oil
200g/7oz minced pork
1 duck egg, beaten
5 Thai shallots, peeled and chopped
1 tsp fish sauce
1 tsp palm sugar
1 tsp light soy sauce
6 medium cleaned whole squid tubes
100ml/3 1/2 fl oz oyster sauce
3 spring onions, trimmed and shredded

1. Crush the peppercorns with garlic and the coriander roots in a mortar to a paste. Heat 1 tbsp oil in a wok and fry the paste for 1–2 minutes until fragrant. Remove from the heat.
2. Mix together the pork mince with the egg and the shallots.
3. Add the fish sauce, sugar and the soy sauce to the paste and mix well. Stir in the pork mixture.
4. Divide the mixture between each squid tube and pack in well to fill. Seal the ends with cocktail sticks. Place over boiling water in a steamer, cover and cook for 10–12 minutes. Remove from the heat and leave to rest for 5 minutes.
5. Heat the remaining oil in a wok. Add the squid to the oil and fry for 1–2 minutes to colour. Drain well and slice. Serve with oyster sauce and shredded spring onions.

Crispy Fried Bream with Three Flavour Sauce

There are many different variations of Three Flavour Sauce. After I have spoken so much about balance and the four elements working in harmony in Thai dishes, this sauce is sweet, sour and salty but not hot. If you want to increase the heat, I suggest that you help yourself to plenty of nam prik, which should always be on the table when food like this is served. Or to really balance the meal overall, serve this with a hot and sour dish such as Hot and Sour Soup with Shellfish (see page 50).
Serves 6

2 tsp chopped garlic
2 tsp chopped Thai shallots
2fl oz vegetable oil
100g/3½oz palm sugar
35ml/7 tsp tamarind water
Juice of 6 limes
1 tbsp fish sauce
2 tsp ginger, julienned
1 long red chilli
5 lime leaves, julienned
4 star anise
6 small bok choy
6 x 175g/6oz bream fillets
20ml/4 tsp chopped coriander
Oil for deep frying

1. Make a paste from half the garlic and half the Thai shallots in a pestle and mortar.
2. Heat the oil in a wok until hot and fry the paste for 1–2 minutes until fragrant.
3. Crumble in the palm sugar and leave to caramelize until a deep red colour, approximately 2–3 minutes.
4. Add the lime juice, tamarind water and fish sauce and bring to a simmer. Then add the ginger, half the chilli and lime leaves and star anise.
5. Cut bok choy in half and steam for 4–5 minutes.
6. Score fish fillet on skin side only in a criss-cross design. Deep fry for 3–4 minutes.
7. Slice and fry remaining chilli, garlic and Thai shallots in a little oil for 1–2 minutes until golden for garnish.

8. To serve, place steamed bok choy on plate, top with fish, spoon over the sauce, sprinkle with the fried garnish and coriander.

Fried Tofu with Pineapple

There was a day when if someone asked me to cook with pineapple I would have jumped up and down and spat my dummy on the floor. I have since matured both mentally and in culinary understanding. Pineapple contains large amounts of pectin and is useful in making a thick sauce such as this one. The fruit shrivels, taking on the appearance and texture of dehydrated pineapple. It provides a great contrast to the softness of the tofu.
Serves 4–6

200g/7oz palm sugar
2 cloves garlic, peeled and pounded in a mortar
1 large red chilli, de-seeded and pounded in a mortar
6 star anise
50ml/2fl oz fish sauce
25ml/5 tsp concentrated tamarind pulp
1 whole pineapple, peeled and chopped into 1cm/½ inch pieces
300g/10½oz fresh firm tofu
Oil for deep frying
A handful Thai basil, deep fried to garnish

1. Place the palm sugar in a large saucepan and add the pounded garlic and chilli and star anise. Heat until the sugar has caramelized and turned golden brown in colour and become aromatic.
2. Add fish sauce, tamarind and a little water to stop the cooking process – check seasoning. Stir well to mix and allow to cool. Then stir in the pineapple.
3. Meanwhile, cut the tofu into 3cm/1½ inch squares. Heat the oil for deep frying in wok until hot and deep fry the tofu for 3–4 minutes. Drain well. To serve, arrange tofu on a serving plate, spoon over the pineapple sauce and top with Thai basil.

Fried Tofu with Pineapple

Crisp Fried Quail and Green Mustard Leaves

Unlike most green vegetables, the green mustard leaf is rather hot. The heat is brought out the more it is cooked, and this makes it a great accompaniment for strong meats such as game. When you buy this cabbage-like plant, make sure that the leaves are very tightly packed and the core thick but not rubbery. Green mustard is seasonal and found in late winter/ early spring. Get hold of it when you can.
Serves 6

2 spring onions, trimmed and finely diced
25ml/2tbsp light soy sauce
6 quails, boned
50g/1^1/$_2$oz potato flour
1 tsp five spice powder
Vegetable oil for deep frying
15g/^{1}/$_2$oz shredded root ginger
200g/7oz green mustard leaves,
split down the centre
15g/^{1}/$_2$oz yellow bean paste
30ml/2 tbsp oyster sauce

1. Place the finely diced spring onions and soy sauce in a large bowl. Add the quails, cover and marinade in the fridge for approximately 24 hours, if possible. Steam for 15 minutes to cook.
2. Mix together the potato flour and the five spice powder.
3. Heat the oil for deep frying in a wok or saucepan. Remove the quails from the marinade and pattern the flour mixture without draining them too much. Place in the oil and deep fry immediately for approximately 4 minutes. Drain on kitchen paper and keep warm whilst preparing the green mustard leaves.
4. Spoon a little of the oil for deep frying – approximately 50ml/2fl oz – into a wok and heat until hot. Add the ginger, the green mustard leaves and the yellow bean paste. Cook well for approximately 3 minutes. Remove from the heat. Stir in the oyster sauce and stand, covered, for 10 minutes, to braise in its own warmth.
5. To serve, arrange braised leaves on serving platter and top with quail.

Squid with Garlic and Peppercorns

Cooking this dish always gives me pleasure. During my trek around Thailand, it was decided that I should prepare this dish in Ko Samui, under the exotic setting of a waterfall. The peppercorns give this dish its heat. They are first crushed and then used with the salt and the flour as a coating. The Portuguese brought chillies into Thailand. Before that peppercorns of all colours were the spicing agent in Thai food.
Serves 2–3

2 dried roasted chillies
30ml/2 tbsp lime juice
5ml/1 tsp palm sugar
2.5ml/^{1}/$_2$ tsp fish sauce
1 whole head garlic, unpeeled
^{1}/$_2$ tsp ground white pepper
Oil for deep frying
15g/^{1}/$_2$oz plain flour
^{1}/$_2$oz cornflour
^{1}/$_2$ tsp ground black pepper
^{1}/$_2$ tsp salt
200g/7oz squid cleaned and scored
1 bunch picked coriander

1. Pound together the dried chillies, lime juice, sugar and fish sauce in a pestle and mortar to form a paste.
2. Pound the whole head of garlic with the white pepper until in small pieces. Heat 1 tbsp oil in a wok until hot and fry the garlic for 1–2 minutes until golden brown. Drain and allow to cool. Set aside.
3. Mix the flours together and season with black pepper and salt. Dust the squid in the flour. Heat the oil for deep frying in a wok until hot then deep fry the squid for about 2 minutes. Drain then mix with the fried garlic and the picked coriander in a bowl and toss. Serve with the chilli dressing.

Squid with Garlic and Peppercorns

Deep Fried Eggs with Sweet Fish Sauce

In a restaurant where I once worked, regulars often used to come in and they would only ever order these most fantastic eggs, known in Thailand as son-in-law eggs. Many dishes have stories attached to them about their origin, and this one has two. The first is that a particular man was so wonderful that his mother-in-law named this dish after him because of its sweet and silky texture. The other is that the man was such a rat that his mother-in-law imagined that the eggs were her son-in-law. First she boiled them, then she peeled them, and after that she plunged them into hot oil until they were blistered. Finally she made a sauce of boiling sugar to pour over them. We'd all like mothers-in-law like that, wouldn't we?
Serves 4–6 as part of a meal

10 large eggs, at room temperature
Oil for deep frying
250g/9oz palm sugar
100ml/3½ fl oz fish sauce
50ml/2fl oz tamarind water
100g/3½oz picked coriander
100g/3½oz crisp fried garnish (see page 25)

1. To cook the eggs, bring a large saucepan of water to the boil. Gently lower the eggs into the boiling water and bring back to the boil – the total cooking process should take no more than 3½ minutes. Drain off the hot water and place the eggs under cold running water until cool. Peel the eggs carefully whilst in the water, taking care not to split them.
2. For the sauce: in a saucepan, combine the palm sugar, fish sauce and tamarind water and simmer until the sugar has dissolved. Skim. Check taste; it should be sweet/sour. DO NOT BOIL. Adjust with palm sugar, fish sauce or tamarind water if necessary.
3. Heat oil for deep frying in a wok and plunge the eggs into the oil. Fry for 5–6 minutes until golden and blistered all over. Drain.
4. To serve: place the eggs in a bowl. Combine the coriander and crisp fried garnish. Mix well. Pour the sauce over eggs and serve, sprinkled with the garnish.

Stir fried Chicken with Bok Choy

The quickest way to get a hot chilli fix is by reheating the curry from the night before. But you might not have one on hand, so the next best thing is to make a quick wok fried dish and drop plenty of raw chillies in at the last minute. Bok choy and choy sum are both Chinese in origin. The word choy means cabbage; the great thing about these cabbages is that they are quick to prepare: just split them and they will only take minutes to cook. Add the leaves as the wok comes off the heat, as this will maintain their crunch.
Serves 4

15g/½oz garlic, peeled
15g/½oz ginger
15g/½oz coriander root
3 boneless, skinless chicken breasts
100ml/3½ fl oz vegetable oil
30ml/2 tbsp fish sauce
2 bok choy
2 choy sum
100ml/3½ fl oz oyster sauce
3 long red chillies, thinly sliced

1. Make a paste from the garlic, ginger and the coriander roots by pounding in a pestle and mortar.
2. Slice the chicken into thin, long strips and set to one side.
3. Heat the wok and add the oil. Reduce the heat and add the paste. Cook slowly, stirring, for 1 minute until fragrant.
4. Add the chicken and cook, stirring, to coat with the paste. Add the fish sauce.
5. Cook for 4–5 minutes until the chicken is cooked. Add the stems of the choys.
6. Drain the excess oil and add the oyster sauce. Cook for 2 minutes until warmed through. Add the leaves of the choys and the chillies. Stir fry for a further minute. Serve.

Stir fried Chicken with Bok Choy

Deep fried Bass

Try to imagine this fish once it has been cooked. The most likely vision to come to mind will be of dragons and deadly sea creatures. With its crisp, scaly skin and its fins protruding up and out in all directions, it is almost as if the whole thing has been frozen in liquid nitrogen and if touched, will shatter and turn to dust. Thankfully it won't. It is not deadly at all, just deadly delicious. If bass is not available then snapper is fairly similar. The fish you use must have a thick skin to hold it together. I'd recommend having your fish gutted through the gills by the fishmonger.
Serves 2–3

2 cloves garlic, peeled and sliced
4 chillies, de-seeded
Bunch coriander, roots trimmed and washed
Salt
Oil for deep frying
20ml/4 tsp palm sugar
10ml/2 tsp tamarind water
Fish sauce to taste
Water
1 kg/2lb 4 oz bass, gutted and scaled
50g/1¾oz crisp fried garnish (see page 25)
Kaffir lime leaves, finely shredded

1. Pound garlic, chillies, coriander roots and salt in a pestle and mortar until fine.
2. Heat 2 tbsp oil in a frying pan or wok and fry off paste for 1–2 minutes until fragrant. Add palm sugar, tamarind water, fish sauce and water. Simmer on a low heat for 5 minutes – it should taste sweet, sour and hot.
3. Rub fish with a little salt and deep fry for 8–10 minutes until cooked.
4. Place fish on a platter and sprinkle over crisp fried garnish and shredded Kaffir lime leaves. Serve with the sauce spooned over.

Omelette Stuffed with Minced Pork

An Asian omelette is not what you might expect. It is cooked in a large amount of oil in a wok and almost deep fried. The oil must be very hot otherwise the egg will soak it all up and make the omelette very greasy. In a Thai meal, an omelette dish is sometimes served to take the heat out of one of the other dishes. A plain omelette may be cooked to serve specifically with a curry instead of rice. This version is filled with minced pork and flavoured with the tart and spicy juice of a Kaffir lime and should be served as part of a main meal. These deep fried omelettes are great filled with crab, minced chicken or vegetables.
Serves 6

Filling
2 tbsp vegetable oil
1 tbsp chopped garlic
60g/2oz chopped onion
225g/8oz ground pork
125g/4½ oz sliced snake beans
2 tbsp fish sauce
125g/4½oz cherry tomatoes, quartered
2 tsp sugar
1 Kaffir lime, juiced
¼ tsp ground black pepper
Handful of chopped coriander
1 Kaffir lime, juiced

Scallops and Black Beans with Coriander

Some of the greatest scallops I have ever eaten have come from just off the coast of Scotland. There, they are found in lochs, where they are grown on ropes and mature in a mix of sea and fresh water. The black beans used to make this sauce can be very salty so be extra vigilant when washing the salt from them, taking into account the environment in which the accompanying scallops have grown. Although more Japanese than Thai, it is worth including this as a mild dish to grace the table.
Serves 6

24 fresh shelled scallops
50ml/2floz peanut oil
100g /3½oz root ginger, peeled and minced
100g/3½oz garlic, peeled and minced
300g/10½oz red onion, peeled and minced
150g/5½oz salted black beans, washed
150g/5½oz Korean hot bean paste
250ml/9floz sho axing cooking wine
200ml/7floz Sake
250ml/9floz Mirin
125g/4½oz rice wine vinegar
30ml/2 tbsp sesame oil
1kg/2lb 4oz Chinese cabbage, unshredded
200g/7oz coriander
150g/5½oz spring onions sliced

1. .Heat half the peanut oil and sweat half minced ginger and garlic, all the onion and black beans in it for 5 minutes. Add Korean hot bean paste and stir fry for 3 minutes.
2. Stir in the cooking wine, Sake, Mirin and rice wine vinegar. Simmer for 35–45 minutes until the alcohol has been cooked out. Remove from the heat and add sesame oil.
3. Sauté remaining garlic and ginger in wok with the remaining peanut oil. Add cabbage and cook until soft.
4. Pan fry the scallops until sealed, then add sauce.
5. To serve, pile cabbage on plates, top with scallops and sauce and sprinkle with coriander and sliced spring onion.

Omelettes

6 large eggs
1 tbsp fish sauce
300ml/½ pt vegetable oil
A handful of picked coriander, to garnish

1. First make the filling. Heat the wok. Add the oil and swirl to coat it until hot. Add the garlic and stir fry for 1 minute until it turns golden brown.
2. Reduce heat and add the onion. Stir fry for 3–4 minutes until softened and then add the pork.
3. Add the beans and fish sauce and toss together. Stir in the tomatoes, sugar and the lime juice. Bring to a simmer and cook for 5–6 minutes until the sauce thickens and then add black pepper and chopped coriander. Set aside and keep warm.
4. Next make the omelettes. Heat the oil in a wok until shimmering. Mix the eggs with fish sauce. Pour half the egg mix into the wok and stir for 30 seconds. Leave to cook for 2 minutes. When the base of the omelette is light brown, turn it over to cook for a few more seconds. Remove and drain well.
5. Place half the pork mixture on top of the omelette and roll it up to form a cigar shape. Repeat the process for the remaining egg and pork mixture.
6. Cut the omelette into 5cm/2 in pieces and serve with picked coriander.

Stir fried Squid with Choy Sum and Tamarind

If each person in the world had only one food they were allowed to eat, then I would have a hard time choosing between scallops and squid. Despite giving it a lot of thought, though, it seems fairly unlikely that I will ever be in the position where I have to make a choice. Choy sum is Chinese. Choy means cabbage, but choy is not at all like the English version. It is bright green with long stems and sometimes, if it is left in the ground too long, it can have small flowers. Beware: the leaves cook very quickly so add them at the very last minute, long after the stems are cooked.
Serves 4

50ml/2fl oz vegetable oil	
400g/14oz squid, cleaned and scored	
300g/10oz choy sum stalks, and flowers	
1 cucumber, halved, seeds removed and sliced	
375g/13oz palm sugar	
25ml/2 tsp tamarind water	
100ml/3½fl oz fish sauce	
1 bunch coriander, picked	
150g/5oz crisp fried garnish (see page 25)	

1. Preheat a medium saucepan or wok over a high flame for 4–5 minutes. Add the oil, carefully followed by the squid. Keep the squid moving so as to make it curl like a flower. This will take about 1 minute.
2. Add choy sum and stir fry for 1–2 minutes until it wilts slightly. Add the cucumber, remove from the heat and toss well. Mix together the sugar, tamarind water and fish sauce, and spoon over a small amount.
3 Place the coriander and fried garnish in a bowl and add a little of the tamarind sauce and mix with a spoon.
4. To serve: arrange squid and choy sum on plates and spoon over the coriander mixture and fried garnish. Serve remaining sauce separately.

Wok fried Beef, Snake Beans and Chilli Paste

When you eat from the street stalls around Thailand, every so often you come across a dish that blows your mind. This is not just because of the spicy heat but sometimes you discover something so delicious and unusual in every way – texture, taste and aroma – that you have to find out how to make it. Eating this dish on a street in Chiang Mai changed the way I thought about all Asian foods. It is soft yet crunchy, hot yet rounded. It has the balance that I've been talking about.
Serves 4–6

Chilli paste

5 dried red long chillies, de-seeded and chopped	
3 red shallots, peeled and chopped	
2 cloves garlic, peeled	
1 stalk lemon grass, sliced	
A small piece galangal, peeled	
5 coriander roots	
1 tsp dried prawns, rinsed	
1 tsp salt	

Beef

100ml/3½fl oz vegetable oil	
300g/10½ oz lean beef, cut into thin strips	
6 snake beans, cut into 7cm/3 inch lengths	
10 lime leaves, torn	
Fish sauce to taste	
A handful Thai basil	
2 red chillies, cut into strips	

1. Combine all the paste ingredients together in a food processor and purée, adding a little oil if needed. Set aside.
2. For the beef heat the oil in the wok. Fry beef in the oil, keeping the heat high for 4–5 minutes, until the outside of the beef is quite crisp.
3. Add snake beans, lime leaves and the chilli paste. Fry for 3–5 minutes until fragrant.
4. Add a little water to moisten, if needed, and season with the fish sauce.
5. Garnish with Thai basil and red chilli strips.

Wok fried Beef, Snake Beans and Chilli Paste

CURRY

To say that the Thais are good at making curries would have to be the understatement of a lifetime. The variety of Thai curries is mind blowing. Originally there were two types of curry – the city curry and the country curry. Now we also have a hybrid known as the suburban curry. The difference between all these curries is the use of coconut milk.

In a country curry there is no coconut milk. The curry paste is cooked in boiling water. In a city curry only coconut milk is used and the paste is cooked in the fat of split coconut milk. In a suburban curry we use both – it's really a country curry which is given a dose of coconut milk to soften its edges.

The other difference between curries is in colour. There are three colours in curry – green curry is made from fresh green chillies, red curry from dried red de-seeded chillies and yellow curry from fresh yellow chillies and turmeric.

A rule of thumb when cooking a curry is to use stronger meats for the country curry so that it can withstand other flavours like pungent, acrid bamboo, which is often used in the water-based curry. When you are cooking a city curry, the initial stages of the process are the most important. Every can of coconut milk on sale in the supermarkets will tell you to shake the can before use but if you are making a curry, DON'T. Separate the contents of the can into two parts – the thick and the thin milk by pouring the thin top layer into a small bowl and setting it aside. Heat the thick milk in a wok or saucepan stirring only occasionally, and it will naturally separate into fat and solids This will take about 5–10 minutes. It is this fat that is used to fry off those wonderfully fragrant pastes that are the backbone of the very best curry.

Have a go at making the paste at home – the difference in flavour is extraordinary and nothing like the pickled, sour stuff that you get in jars. There will always be too much paste for one dish, so once it has been cooked, allow the excess to cool and then keep it refrigerated in a screw top jar. It should keep for a week.

Thick Beef and Peanut Curry

Green Curry with Chicken and Sweet Potato

The most common mistake made with Thai curries is that people leave them to boil for too long and destroy the individual flavours. As with the rest of Thai cooking, most of the time is spent at the preparation stage. Use meat or fish of the best quality and, contrary to many people's beliefs, the time in the wok or the pot is not long at all. Skinless and boneless chicken is used in a green curry. Try the thigh meat as it won't dry out. From start to finish most curries should take less than 25 minutes.

Serves 4–6

Green Curry paste

1/2 tsp coriander seeds, roasted
1 tsp cumin seeds, roasted
100g/3 1/2oz large green chillies, chopped
15g/1/2oz small green chillies, chopped
15g/1/2oz lemon grass, stripped
1 Thai shallot, peeled
15g/1/2oz garlic, peeled
A small piece galangal, peeled
4 coriander roots
15g/1/2oz white pepper
10ml/2 tsp shrimp paste
5ml/1 tsp salt
30g/1oz Thai basil, picked
30g/1oz fresh coriander, picked

Curry

300ml/1/2 pt thick coconut milk
40g/1 1/2oz palm sugar
15ml/1 tbsp fish sauce
300g/10 1/2oz sweet potato, peeled and cut into small cubes
500ml/18fl oz thin coconut milk
500g/1lb 2oz chicken thigh fillet, cut into small pieces
6 Japanese aubergines, halved
1kg/2lb 4oz snake beans, cut into short lengths
3 lime leaves, finely shredded
3 long red chillies, finely shredded

1. First make the curry paste. Grind the roasted coriander and cumin seeds in a mortar to form a powder.
2. Place the remaining paste ingredients in a food processor and blend until smooth. Add the spice powder, blend again until smooth and set aside.
3. Now prepare the curry. Heat the thick coconut milk over a medium heat until the milk splits.
4. Add 2 tbsp of the prepared green curry paste and fry for 3–4 minutes until fragrant.
5. Add the palm sugar and fish sauce, and cook for 2 minutes. Stir in the sweet potato and the thin coconut milk.
6. Bring to the boil and cook for 5 minutes. Add the chicken, aubergines and snake beans and cook for a further 5 minutes until tender and cooked through. Serve garnished with julienne lime leaves and chillies.
Note: Store remaining curry paste in a screw-top jar in the fridge for up to 1 week.

Typical Thai curry

Monkfish Curry

Many books will start with the common curry and the ones which are known as favourites, but I want to start with a real curry, which typifies Thai food at its very best. A jungle curry should be as sour as it is hot. The further north you are, the hotter the curry. It is only in recent times and in the grand courts that large quantities of meat and fish were added to curries. The dish itself should be soupy with lots of liquid to be absorbed by rice. It also means it is pretty cheap to make. Use smoked haddock if you can't get monkfish.
Serves 4

Country curry paste

23 white peppercorns, ground
2 tsp salt
50g/1oz green chillies, half de-seeded
11 Thai shallots, peeled and chopped
11 cloves garlic, peeled and chopped
1 stalk lemon grass, peeled and finely sliced
40g/1½oz galangal, peeled and sliced
9 coriander roots
Grated rind of 1 lime
60g/2oz krachai root, peeled and sliced, (optional)
20 ml/4 tsp roasted shrimp paste

Curry

150ml/¼ pt fish sauce
1kg/2lb 4oz monkfish fillet, cut into bite-sized pieces
2 litres/3½ pt chicken stock
100ml/3½fl oz Thai whisky
200g/7oz snake beans, cut into short pieces
200g/7oz bamboo shoots, cut into small pieces
1 bunch Thai basil
30 Kaffir lime leaves, torn

1. First make the curry paste. Grind the white peppercorns to form a powder in a pestle and mortar.
2. Transfer to a food processor and add all the rest of the ingredients and blend quickly to make a paste, adding no liquid. Set aside.
3. In a saucepan heat 100ml/3½fl oz water over a high heat. Add the 4 tbsp prepared curry paste. Stir for a few minutes, cooking until fragrant. Add the fish sauce and continue to cook for another minute.
4. Add the monkfish and cook for 1–2 minutes until sealed. Pour in the stock. Bring to the boil and simmer for 1–2 minutes.
5. Add the remaining ingredients. Simmer for another minute. Leave to steam for 5 minutes before serving.
Note: Store remaining curry paste in a screw-top jar, well sealed, in the fridge for up to 1 week.

Prawn Red Curry

In the sun-drenched south, where coconut milk is in abundance and the sea yields huge salty prawns, this curry is served to many visitors. When cooking this at home, don't wash the prawns as their rich salty flavour is an integral part of the dish.
Serves 4-6

Red curry paste

10 red dried chillies
30g/1oz coriander roots
4 lime leaves, cut en julienne
2 stalks lemon grass
50g/1³⁄₄oz galangal, peeled and sliced
1 tbsp grated rind Kaffir lime
30g/1oz sliced Thai shallots
30g/1oz sliced garlic
Salt
15 ml/1 tbsp shrimp paste
½ tsp coriander seeds, roasted and ground
¼ tsp cumin seed, roasted and ground
A small piece mace, roasted and ground
5 white peppercorns, roasted and ground

Curry

500ml/18fl oz thick coconut milk
30ml/2 tbsp palm sugar
15ml/1 tbsp fish sauce
500g/1lb 2oz pumpkin, peeled, seeded and
chopped, and rinsed twice
2 litres/3½ pt thin coconut milk
30 large raw prawns, cleaned, shelled, leaving
the tail intact
2 long red chillies, sliced
Lime leaves to garnish, torn

1. First make the curry paste. In a food processor, blend the chillies with the coriander roots, lime leaves, lemon grass, galangal, lime rind, shallots and garlic, and add a little salt. Add shrimp paste and blend to a smooth paste. Add a little water, if needed.

2. Grind roasted spices and peppercorns in a mortar and mix into the paste.

3. Now make the curry. Place the thick coconut milk in a wok and heat, stirring, it until it splits . Add 4 tbsp paste and cook, stirring constantly, over a medium heat for 5 minutes until fragrant.

4. Add the palm sugar and bring to a simmer, then add the fish sauce.

5. Stir in the pumpkin and cook for 1 minute. Pour in the thin coconut milk. Simmer for 12–15 minutes until pumpkin is soft.

6. Add prawns and cook for 1–2 minutes longer until they are just cooked. The curry should be sweet and creamy. Add chillies. Transfer to serving bowls and garnish with lime leaves.

Sour Yellow Curry with Vegetables

Sour Yellow Curry with Vegetables

A yellow curry should be as sour as it is hot. The beauty of a vegetable curry is that anything within reason can be added to make the dish complete. Cooking vegetables for curry can be difficult. Too much cooking and you get a mushy sludge and too little and you end up with lots of hard bullets. The vegetables will take on the flavours from the paste very quickly. If they are left to cook for too long the natural vegetable flavours can be overtaken by the flavours of the stock in which they are simmered.
Serves 6

Yellow curry paste

200g/7oz long yellow chillies, de-seeded and chopped
6 red shallots
3 cloves of garlic, peeled and chopped
50g/1³/₄oz galangal
2 tsp salt
2 tsp fried shrimp paste
30g/1oz dried shrimps
15g/¹/₂oz fresh turmeric

Curry

300ml/¹/₂ pt vegetable stock or water
Pinch of salt
2 tsp sugar
4 tbsp thick tamarind water
300g/10¹/₂oz snake beans, cut at an angle into short lengths
500g/1lb 2oz potato, peeled and diced
500g/1lb 2oz pumpkin, peeled, de-seeded and diced
500g/1lb 2oz sweet potato, peeled and diced
30ml/2 tbsp fish sauce
200g/7oz bean sprouts
100g/3¹/₂oz sugar snap peas, topped and tailed
3 Chinese cabbage leaves, shredded

1. To make the curry paste, blend all the ingredients together in a pestle and mortar and set aside.
2. For the curry, in a medium pan combine the stock or water, salt, sugar and tamarind water. Bring to the boil.

3. Add the snake beans, potato, pumpkin and sweet potato and simmer in the liquor for 5–6 minutes. Add the sugar snap peas and cook for a further 2 minutes. Drain, reserving the stock, and refresh the vegetables in cold water and keep to one side.
4. Heat the oil in a wok and fry 60g/2oz prepared curry paste for 1 minute. Add the reserved stock. Season with fish sauce.
5. To serve: return the vegetables to the stock, along with the cabbage and bean sprouts. Bring to the boil, simmer for 2 minutes to heat through and serve. Add more tamarind water and fish sauce if necessary.

Green Curry Vegetables and Tamarind

Pungent, sour, salty and hot, this recipe is the winner from this chapter. It is still widely thought that red curry is the hot one and green is milder. This is untrue. Green curry paste is made with fresh chillies and their hot seeds whereas a red curry paste is made with re-hydrated long red or serrano chillies and all the seeds are removed prior to pounding.
Serves 6–8

Cooking broth

2 tsp salt
20 g/¾oz fresh turmeric
150g/5½oz tamarind pulp

Sauce

1 tbsp vegetable oil
200ml/7fl oz thick coconut milk
4 tbsp green curry paste (see page 104)
40g/1½oz palm sugar
15ml/1 tbsp fish sauce
300ml/½ pt thin coconut milk

Curry:

100g/3½oz Japanese aubergines, halved
100g/3½oz sweet potato, peeled and cut into cubes
100g/3½oz pumpkin, peeled and cut into 2.5cm/1 inch pieces
100g/3½oz bok choy, halved
100g/3½oz fresh bamboo, sliced
100g/3½oz pea aubergines
100g/3½oz snake beans, cut into short lengths
100g/3½oz spring onions, cut into 7cm/3 in pieces
100g/31/2 oz sugar snap peas, topped and tailed

1. Blend salt, turmeric and tamarind pulp into a paste in preparation for the main dish.
2. In a large saucepan combine paste with 3 litres/5pints water. Bring to the boil to make a cooking broth.
3. Poach the vegetables for the curry individually in the cooking broth for 4–5 minutes or until cooked and set aside.
4. For the sauce, heat 2 tsp of the vegetable

oil in a wok together with the thick coconut milk until almost toasted.
5. Add the curry paste and fry for 1-2 minutes until fragrant.
6. Add the palm sugar, fish sauce and the thin coconut milk and bring to the boil.
7. Add the poached vegetables to the sauce and warm through, and season with fish sauce.

Lobster Curry

In Thailand lobster curry is made for tourists and would not normally be found on any street market stall as a lunchtime snack. Some are very good and this dish shows how the Thais have adapted their food to visitors' tastes. But to really eat, the streets are where the action is.
Serves 4

Curry

200ml/7fl oz thick coconut milk
30g/1 tbsp red curry paste (see page 97)
5 ml/1 tbsp palm sugar
Fish sauce to taste
400ml/14fl oz thin coconut milk
1 kg/2 lb 4oz lobster
50 g/1¾oz plain flour
Vegetable oil for deep frying
100g/3½oz rice vermicelli (khanom jin)
2 long red chillies, finely shredded
Picked coriander, to garnish

1. Heat the thick coconut milk in a wok over a medium heat until it splits.
2. Add the curry paste and fry for 1–2 minutes until fragrant.
3. Add the palm sugar and fish sauce, and cook for 2 minutes. Stir in the thin coconut milk and bring to the boil. Remove from the heat and set aside.
4. Cut the lobster into pieces and crack the claws. Coat with seasoned flour. Heat the oil for deep frying in a wok until hot and fry the lobster for 2–3 minutes until golden and cooked.
5. Deep fry noodles for 2–3 minutes until crisp and drain.
6. Arrange lobster on plate; mix the noodles with some of the chillies and coriander and place on top of the lobster.
7. Spoon the sauce on and around the lobster to serve.

Steamed Fish Curry

Comfort food exists in all countries. For Thais it has to be rice and sweet sago puddings covered with palm sugar and finished off with condensed milk. This steamed fish curry is a savoury comfort food. Comparable with the most succulent fish cake ever eaten, you get the added bonus of warm lime-scented coconut milk on the top. The freshness of the fish is paramount. This curry will turn to a sludge not dissimilar to over-cooked scrambled egg, if the fish is old. In Asia, steamed fish curry is served in banana skin boats, held together with wood skewers, but sometimes I resort to the stapler. *Makes 12*

1kg/2lb 4oz skinless, meaty white fish fillets, sliced
1tbsp red curry paste (see page 97)
2 eggs
9 lime leaves, torn
5ml/1 tsp oyster sauce
5ml/1 tsp fish sauce
500ml/18fl oz canned coconut milk, shaken
4 leaves Thai basil, shredded
2 red chillies, finely shredded
4 sprigs coriander
4 banana leaf boats (see note below)

1. Place three quarters of the fish in a food processor. Add the red curry paste, eggs and lime leaves, oyster sauce, and fish sauce and blend until smooth. Transfer to a large bowl and mix in the remaining sliced fish and three quarters of the coconut milk.

2. Sprinkle the basil in the banana leaf boats and place 2tbsp of the mix on top of the basil. Top each with a sprig of coriander, chilli and 1 tbsp of the remaining coconut milk. Place in a steamer over simmering water and steam for 8 minutes until cooked through. Be careful not to make the mix too dry. Too much egg will make it rubbery and not enough coconut milk will make it dry.

Note: to make banana boats, cut rounds from the banana leaves. Bring a large saucepan of water to the boil and blanch the leaves for 2–3 minutes. Drain well. Cut four equal incisions evenly around each banana circle to within 5cm/2in of the middle, fold in the flaps and pin with cocktail sticks to form a small basket/boat shape.

Red Chicken and Bamboo Curry

Take a boat heading south up the river that flows through the centre of Bangkok. Turn left just after the massive fresh fruit and vegetable market, Pak Klong Talat, and follow the little klong for a good 45 minutes. Around there somewhere is a place called the Thai House, owned by Khun Pip who teaches farangs like me how to cook. If the chance arises and the word is out that Khun Pip is cooking Red Chicken and Bamboo Curry just follow your nose, it is too good to be true.

Paste

10 dried large red chillies, re-hydrated and de-seeded
50g/1¾oz galangal, peeled
1 stalk lemon grass
Finely grated rind of 1 lime
10 coriander roots
7 cloves garlic, peeled
3 Thai shallots, peeled
11 white peppercorns
1 tsp shrimp paste

Curry

500ml/18fl oz thick coconut milk
500g/1lb 2oz boneless, skinless chicken, cut into small pieces
10 lime leaves
30ml/2 tbsp palm sugar
750ml/1¼ pt thin coconut milk
300g/10½oz fresh bamboo, sliced
45ml/3tbsp fish sauce
A handful Thai basil
A handful bean sprouts
A handful coriander

1. First make the paste. Place the chillies in a bowl and cover with warm water. Soak for 30 minutes, then drain and de-seed. Pound all the paste ingredients in a pestle and mortar until smooth, or blend in a food processor without any liquid. Set aside.
2. Now make the curry. Heat the thick coconut milk in a wok until it splits (evaporates) and fry 3 tbsp of the prepared paste for 1–2 minutes until fragrant.
3. Add the chicken, lime leaves and the palm

Indonesian Red Curry Paste

10 dried large red chillies
11 white peppercorns
1/2 tsp coriander seeds
1/2 tsp cumin seeds
1 piece mace
3 Thai shallots, peeled
7 cloves garlic, peeled
1 stalk lemon grass
50g/1¾oz galangal, peeled
Finely grated rind of 1 lime
10 coriander roots

Curry

500ml/18fl oz thick coconut milk
5ml/1 tsp shrimp paste
15ml/1 tbsp palm sugar
750ml/1¼ pt thin coconut milk
15 lime leaves
Handful roast peanuts, crushed
700g/1lb 9oz thinly sliced beef fillet
A few Thai basil leaves
A few coriander leaves
45 ml/3 tbsp fish sauce
3 long red chillies, sliced

105

sugar and cook for 2 minutes until the chicken is well coated. Pour in the thin coconut milk and stir in the bamboo. Season with the fish sauce and bring to the boil. Cook for a further 6–7 minutes. Taste and re-season if necessary.
4. Serve with the basil stirred in at the last minute, and the bean sprouts and coriander on top.

Thick Beef and Peanut Curry

Thick sweet curries have made their way to Thailand via the people of Malaysia, Singapore and Indonesia. They are the seriously rich curries and small amounts will suffice. Eating rice with this sort of curry as well as the peanuts, could be a little too much. You may find a deep fried plain omelette on your table with a curry like this. It is seasoned with a pinch of sugar and salt or fish sauce. This is the way Thais eat thick curries.
Serves 4–6

1. First make the paste. Place the chillies in a bowl and cover with warm water. Soak for 30 minutes, then drain and de-seed. Meanwhile, rinse the peppercorns, coriander and cumin seeds, place in cold water, and dry with a cloth. In a heavy based frying pan, roast the spices over a medium flame until the cumin darkens. Cool slightly, then grind to a powder in a pestle and mortar.
2. Pound the chillies and add remaining ingredients and blend to a paste. Set aside.
3. For the curry, heat the thick coconut milk in a wok until it splits and add 3 tbsp of the prepared paste. Cook for 5 minutes until fragrant and then add the palm sugar, cook out for 6–8 minutes until the paste is rich reddish brown and caramelized.
4. Add the thin coconut milk, lime leaves and shrimp paste. Bring to the boil, add the peanuts and then the beef. Cook for a further 2–3 minutes. Remove from the heat and stir in the basil and coriander leaves. Taste and season with fish sauce and finish with chopped red chillies.

5
GRILLED AND BARBECUED

When we think of grilling, we probably visualize the part of the oven where we cook toast or grill sausages. Well, it's not quite like that in Thailand, where grilling takes place in a metre-long metal box that looks similar to a window box. Imagine it on the side of a road, full of glowing charcoals and covered with strips of wire. On top of the wire, there could be satay sizzling, sending out little flashes as the fat renders itself away. Alternatively, there could be traveller's chicken, with its skin crisp and blistered, ready to be served with sweet chilli sauce or chopped peanuts and cucumber.

Or your grill could be somewhere in the jungle, not far from the river. If you find yourself near the border with Burma, you would be grilling on a 44 gallon drum, cut in half and filled with coal. Whole suckling pigs and big meat joints could well have been marinated in fish sauce and coconut milk for a number of hours, the delicious smoky smell indicating when the food was ready to serve.

You realize this means that your home barbecue should, from this day forward, no longer consist of just sausages and burgers. So take the coals out of the cupboard or chop up the wood to be burnt and, for the very best flavour, get set to barbecue.

Don't start cooking until you have glowing embers. If you need to add more fuel to the barbecue, put the food to one side until it reaches the right temperature. The fat from the food will turn to oil when it is melted by the heat and this will fuel most coal and wood fires. It is very important, when you grill or barbecue, to rub any extra oil onto the food and not onto the grill. For recipes such as Grilled Guinea Fowl and Pomelo, you don't need any extra oil as the coconut milk has its own fat. The same is true for the recipe for Spice-crusted Bream and Yogurt.

Food for grilling and barbecuing is best when cooked slowly as this allows for the flavours to be released. The meat has to have time to tenderize. If meat or fish cooks too quickly, it will shrivel up and become tough.

Traveller's Chicken

Barbecued Pork Ribs

Pork fat is really something of great beauty and flavour. I know that many people just hate the idea of eating fat in any way, shape or form, so this recipe will work with those funny bones that butchers call spare ribs. Beef can also be substituted for pork but to me the flavour of pork cannot be topped. If you are using the belly, as the recipe suggests, then let the pork cook for a long time on the grill. This gives the meat time to absorb the fat as it melts.
Serves 8

Pork

6 cloves garlic, peeled
10 white peppercorns
10 coriander roots
50ml/2fl oz blended sesame oil
300ml/½pt ketchup manis
2kg/4lb 8oz short pork spare ribs

Peanut sauce

25ml/5 tsp thick coconut milk15ml/1 tbsp red curry paste (see page 97)
5ml/1 tsp fish sauce
15ml/1 tbsp palm sugar
60ml/4 tbsp tamarind water
150g/5½oz roasted peanuts, chopped
100ml/3½fl oz thin coconut milk

1. In a pestle and mortar, crush the garlic, peppercorns and coriander roots to form a paste and mix them with the sesame oil and the ketchup manis.
2. To cook, barbecue the pork ribs over hot coals or wood for 20–25 minutes, turning every 3 minutes, until tender and cooked through.
3. Meanwhile make the peanut sauce to serve with the ribs. In a saucepan, combine the thick coconut milk and red curry paste and cook for 5 minutes on low heat. Add the fish sauce, palm sugar, tamarind water and chopped peanuts and cook for a further 5 minutes. Add the thin coconut milk and set aside until required.

Grilled Lemon Grass Beef

Some people could mistake lemon grass beef for satay. The real satay comes from the countries neighbouring Thailand, but the Thais have a grilled beef dish which is quite similar. Grilled lemon grass beef is the type of dish found on street market stalls throughout Thailand. Most stallholders own a cart with a few very small boxes filled with coal that is always hot. The grill is in constant use and always ready for hungry customers.
Serves 6-–8

1 stalk lemon grass
1 clove of garlic, peeled and finely chopped
1 shallot, peeled and finely chopped
1 Bird's Eye chilli, finely chopped
30ml/2 tbsp fish sauce
15ml/1 tbsp lime juice
15ml/1 tbsp roasted sesame oil
15ml/1 tbsp dry-roasted sesame seeds
1kg/1lb 4oz lean sirloin beef, trimmed and sliced thinly against the grain

1. Place all the above ingredients in a food processor, except the beef, with 1 tbsp water. Process to make a paste.
2. Place the beef in a shallow dish and mix in the paste. Cover and chill for 1 hour to tenderize. Cook on barbecue over hot coals or on a grill plate for 3 minutes on each side.
3. Serve with rice paper, spring onions and bean sprouts accompanied by peanut dipping sauce.

Grilled Lemon Grass Beef

Sweet and Sour Grilled Prawns

The Aussie barbie just wouldn't be the same without the shrimp. We Aussies understand the shrimp to be very small, the sort of thing that goes into a sandwich with Marie Rose sauce. So when I talk about prawns, I don't mean the little ones that come 300 to a kilo but the really big ones. A useful guideline for choosing prawns is the quantity to weight. Look for 16–20 per pound and if you are lucky enough to see the fresh ones with the heads on, they are the best that you can buy.
Serves 4

Dressing
60g/2oz palm sugar
2 tbsp lime juice
2 tbsp fish sauce
1 tbsp tamarind water

Salad
20 whole medium raw prawns
6 Thai shallots, peeled and finely sliced lengthwise
1 stalk lemon grass, sliced into small rings
5 Kaffir lime leaves, sliced finely
A small piece of young ginger, finely shredded
1/2 red chilli, de-seeded, finely shredded
2 tbsp picked fresh coriander leaves
Mint leaves, for garnish

1. Put the palm sugar, lime juice, fish sauce and tamarind water in a small saucepan. Bring to a simmer but do not boil. Stir to dissolve the sugar. Remove from the heat and set aside.
2. Now prepare the salad. Cook the prawns on the barbecue over hot coals or in a griddle pan for 1–2 minutes on each side until pink and cooked through. Put all the remaining ingredients for the salad in a bowl. Add the prepared dressing and drop the grilled prawns in whilst still hot. Mix together and serve on a banana leaf.

Spice-crusted Bream and Yogurt

This has to be one of the only recipes in the book containing any dairy produce. Thais do not eat dairy foods so it is obvious that this recipe is not Thai or from China, but was inspired by the Indians. The yogurt performs the same process as fish sauce and coconut milk – tenderizing and breaking down the flesh. It also acts as a protective barrier that turns sweet when exposed to high heat, in just the same way as coconut milk does.
Serves 2--3

1x1kg/2lb 4oz whole sea bream, scaled and gutted
1 bunch picked coriander

Spiced Crust
2 medium onions, peeled and chopped
10ml/2 tsp chopped ginger
1 tsp chopped garlic
1 tsp chilli powder
1/2 tsp turmeric powder
1 tsp paprika
1 tsp garam masala
1 tsp cardamom
5 long red chillies, chopped
200ml/7fl oz natural yogurt
Juice of 1 lime

1. Place the fish in a shallow dish. Cut 4–5 splits in each side of it. Fill the cavity with coriander.
2. Blend all the Spiced Crust ingredients together to form a smooth paste.
3. Cover the whole fish in paste and marinate in fridge for 24 hours.
4. Grill the fish over hot coals or on the grill plate for 6-8 minutes on each side until dark and serve with rice.

Fish Steak in Coconut Sauce

Although I am a firm believer in leaving the best ingredients alone and letting them speak for themselves, the simple task of rubbing a fish with a marinade can make a huge difference. The bigger fish derive the most benefit from this type of treatment.
Serves 4–6

60ml/4 tbsp vegetable oil
3 medium onions, peeled and sliced
10 cloves garlic, peeled and crushed
100g/3½oz shredded coconut
10ml/2 tsp chilli powder
3 tbsp ground coriander
10ml/2 tsp ground cumin
2.5ml/½ tsp turmeric
1 tbsp white poppy seeds, crushed
20ml/4 tsp tamarind pulp
1.2kg/2½lb fish steaks such as cod, snapper, kingfish or swordfish
Salt
Fresh coriander leaves to garnish

1. Heat the oil in a wok and gently fry the onion and garlic in a pan until golden. Add the coconut and fry for 1–2 minutes, stirring to prevent burning. Cool slightly then blend in a food processor to form a smooth paste.
2. Return the paste to the wok and add all the spices and poppy seeds and fry for a second or so.
3. Mix tamarind with 500ml/18fl oz water then strain into the wok. Bring to the boil and simmer for 5 minutes. Add the fish and simmer gently for 5–6 minutes until it is cooked through. Taste and adjust seasoning with salt.
4. Serve with rice and garnish with picked coriander leaves.

Roast Sea Bass in Banana Leaf with Sambal

An evening meal in Singapore is never served without sambal, a strong paste that has many variations but is always hot and adds a nice kick to grilled fish. Once again, this dish is not of Thai origin, but is cooked in the south where the country borders Malaysia. Wrapping the fish in a banana leaf, before cooking it in the wok is also evidence of the southern influence. The banana leaf imparts a nutty, smoky flavour and protects the fish's delicate flesh; in fact the fish literally steams inside its leafy chamber.
Serves 4–6

Sambal
200g/7oz galangal, peeled
30g/1oz root turmeric
25 Long red dried chilli, cleaned and re-hydrated
5 candlenuts
50g/1¾oz black shrimp paste
250g/9oz Thai shallots, peeled
7 stalks of lemon grass
A handful fresh coriander
Fish sauce to taste
1 lime leaf, finely shredded
60ml/4 tbsp vegetable oil

Fish
1 whole sea bass, scaled and gutted.
Salt and white pepper
1 large banana leaf

1. First make the sambal. Blend all the ingredients except the oil in a food processor until smooth. Heat the oil in a wok and fry the paste over low heat for 30 minutes. Set aside.
2. For the fish, preheat the oven to 190°C/375°F/Gas 5. Place 2 tbsps sambal and seasoning in centre of fish. Season outside of fish.
3. Cut out the stringy backbone from the banana leaf and keep to one side. Roll bass in the leaf at an angle until fish is covered. Tuck in ends then tie with the reserved banana string. Bake in oven for 20 minutes until cooked through. Serve with rice.

Grilled Guinea Fowl and Pomelo

Guinea fowl is extremely underrated. Many people believe that the guinea fowl is very stringy in flavour and has virtually no meat content. This is absolutely untrue. Guinea fowl is not that far away from a good free range chicken and the meat content is high; every part of the bird can be eaten without finding any tough and stringy pieces.
Serves 4–5

2 x 1kg/2lb 4oz guinea fowl
400ml/14fl oz thick coconut milk
100ml/3½fl oz fish sauce
4 slices galangal
2 stalks lemon grass
12 lime leaves

1. Split the guinea fowl down the centre by removing the backbone and place in a shallow dish. Pour over the coconut milk and fish sauce. Cover and chill for 12 hours, turning the guinea fowl occasionally.
2. Pound the galangal and the lemon grass with the lime leaves in the mortar to release the flavour. Add the pounded mix to the coconut milk and leave to infuse for a few hours, turning the guinea fowl occasionally.
3. Heat the barbecue. Drain the guinea fowl and grill over coals for about 25–30 minutes, turning, until cooked through. Leave to rest for 20 minutes whilst preparing the salad and dressing.

Salad
2 pomelo, peeled and segmented
A handful of Thai basil
4 pieces pak chee laos
1 green mango, peeled, and shredded

Dressing
6 cloves garlic, peeled
4 shallots, peeled
100g/3½oz palm sugar
10 green chillies, 8 de-seeded
4 coriander roots
½ stick lemon grass
30ml/2 tbsp fish sauce
100ml/3½fl oz lime juice

4. In a pestle and mortar, pound the garlic, shallots, chillies, coriander roots and lemon grass to a paste. Add the palm sugar and crush again to a paste. Add the lime juice and fish sauce to taste.
5. To serve, sprinkle the dressing over the salad and serve with the guinea fowl.

Grilled Guinea Fowl and Pomelo

Seared Salmon and Green Mango Salad

In the north of Thailand, the night market stalls grill dried fish, which has spent its final days shrivelling in the sun. Its flavour is intense and the flesh slightly oily. If this appeals, try this recipe, putting the salmon on the barbecue when it is just about to settle. The smoke produced by the dripping natural oils calms the intensity of the fish and the salad gives it sweetness and rounds off the flavours. Salmon is not found in Asia as the waters are too warm for it to survive, but it is good as a change with this salad.
Serves 4

75g/2³⁄₄oz chopped garlic
200g/7oz long red chilli, de-seeded and finely shredded
100g/3¹⁄₂oz cherry tomatoes, halved
100g/3¹⁄₂oz snake beans, cut into small rounds
¹⁄₂ bunch coriander, root chopped and the leaves picked
200g/7oz shredded green papaya
200g/7oz shredded green mango
20ml/4 tsp chopped roasted shrimps
700g/1lb 9oz skinless salmon fillets

Dressing

3 small green chillies, pounded in a mortar	
20ml/4 tsp lime juice	
20ml/4 tsp tamarind water	
20ml/4 tsp palm sugar	
10ml/2 tsp light soy sauce	

1. For the salad, mix all ingredients together in a large bowl, except the salmon. Cover and chill until required.
2. Brush the salmon with oil and place on a barbecue over hot coals or wood or a grill plate and cook until very dark, then turn over.
It will take about 15 minutes to cook through.
3. In a mortar and pestle mix all the ingredients for the dressing together with 2 tsp water and then pour into the salad.
4. Serve the salad with the salmon.

Traveller's Chicken

On every street corner in every market place in Bangkok you will find this type of chicken being cooked. For some reason, travellers are happy to eat barbecued chicken from the streets, even when they have been scared to eat many other things. The versatility of the paste

in this recipe means it can be adapted for quail and guinea fowl. Take time with the cooking and keep the skin intact so that the chicken flesh is well looked after. The outside of the bird should be dark and almost charred. It's particularly wonderful when eaten with sweet chilli sauce in the heat of a Bangkok street, with the juices dripping down your arm.
Serves 4

20 white peppercorns
6 coriander roots
1 bulb garlic, peeled
15ml/1 tbsp fish sauce
50ml/2fl oz tamarind water
50g/1¾oz palm sugar
1.5kg/3lb 8oz chicken, cut into 8 joints

1. Crush the peppercorns in a pestle and mortar. Add the rest of the ingredients except the chicken and pound to form a paste.
2. Score the chicken skin so that each piece has a number of incisions and place in a shallow dish. Rub the chicken with the paste, cover and leave to marinate in the fridge overnight.
3. The next day, heat the barbecue until the embers are smoking and place the chicken pieces on the outside of the grill rack so that the chicken heats slowly – this helps the flavour to mature and the skin to stay intact – it will take about 20 minutes.
4. Transfer the chicken to the hottest part of the coals and cook for a further 5 minutes to seal and crisp.
5. Eat from the bone with chilli sauce (see page 58) and shredded green mango.

6
PASTES, SAUCES AND RELISHES

Nam phriks or chilli pastes and dips are very important parts of a Thai meal, and using them means that the balancing act essential to the philosophy of Thai cooking can really achieved. Although these dips and sauces are only served in small quantities, they take a long time to prepare. The highly concentrated flavours are achieved by blending together several fiery ingredients.

Once you have mastered making your own nam phrik, you won't resort to the takeaway quite so often as you will have mastered one of the essentials of Thai cooking. To never visit your local Thai takeaway would be a sin because the best way to learn is from the experts, but the more knowledgeable you become, then the better choices you will make.

Pad phriks and their cousin, the relish, come in many forms, from salty duck to pork with tomatoes and to the all-amazing chilli jam. There are many variations of these dips and sauces because they are regional and seasonally dependent. Most are quite hot and are eaten with raw vegetables, or in small amounts as a condiment or for extra flavouring. Their versatility means that they are hard to pigeonhole.

Chilli Jam

Chilli Jam

Chilli Jam comes in many shapes, forms, colours, textures and consistencies. The one ingredient common to all is the large red dried chillies, available in all good Thai shops and from your local Chinatown. If the fresh red chilli is used, it will not give the right colour and flavour intensity and it also holds too much water, preventing the jam from reaching the thick sticky consistency that is needed. Chilli Jam should be a rich, dark red colour and although it takes a long time to cook, the end result can be stored in the fridge for about a week. The oil that the chillies are cooked in is great for stir frying.

Makes 400g/14oz

15g/½oz dried chillies
400ml/14fl oz vegetable oil
150g/5½diced red pepper
125g/4½oz chopped Spanish onion
150g/5½oz cherry tomatoes – halved
2 tsp sliced garlic
50g/1¾oz dried shrimp
30g/1oz palm sugar
125ml/4fl oz fish sauce

1. Soak the chillies for 15 minutes in warm water, then drain and remove the seeds. Heat the oil in a wok until hot, deep fry the chillies for 1–2 minutes until dark red and crisp. Drain well.
2. Heat 50ml/2fl oz oil in another wok and fry the pepper, onion and garlic for 2–3 minutes. Stir in the tomatoes and chillies, and cook gently for 30 minutes.

3. Reheat the oil for deep frying and deep fry the shrimp for 1 minute, drain and add to the tomato and chilli mixture.

4. Drain off the excess oil from the tomato and chilli mixture then put in a food processor and blend until smooth. Slowly add the palm sugar and fish sauce to taste. Cook out on stove for 1 hour on a low heat, stirring to prevent drying and burning.

5. The jam should be dark in colour – well caramelized and balanced in flavour and seasoned appropriately.

Note: To make this recipe in such large quantities may be extravagant but it keeps for such a long time and is so versatile that it has to be done.

Pork and Peanut Relish

Addiction is a great thing when it refers to Thai food. There's something in this dish which keeps you yearning for more. Whether it is the chilli or the sugar I am not sure, but I know that pork and peanut relish is a combination guaranteed to spark off an addiction in even the most abstemious of people. Make only the smallest amount.
Makes 80g/2½oz

45ml/3 tbsp peanut oil
2 cloves garlic, peeled and finely chopped
30ml/2 tbsp lean ground pork
5ml/1 tsp chilli paste (see page 90)
15ml/1 tbsp fish sauce
15ml/1 tbsp unsalted peanut butter
5ml/1 tsp caster sugar
45g/1½oz roasted unsalted peanuts

1. Heat the oil in a wok and add the garlic. Fry for 1 minute until lightly browned. Add the pork, stir well and lower the heat. Add the chilli paste and fish sauce.

2. Mix the peanut butter with 250ml/8fl oz warm water and add to the sauce. Stir well then add the sugar. Lower the heat and cook for 2 minutes, stirring all the time. Sprinkle with the roasted peanuts.

Roast Chillies and Sweet Pork Relish

Only a very confident culture and a real food master could have thought up this amazing sweet pork relish. I remember people in markets buying, not sugar-coated peanuts, but sugar-coated pork. It is a true reflection of the power of fish sauce and its ability to make almost anything taste good.
Serves 10 as accompaniment

100ml/3½fl oz vegetable oil
1kg/2lb 4oz cooked boneless pork cut into 1cm (½ inch cubes)
300g/10½oz caster sugar
50ml/2fl oz light soy sauce
200ml/7fl oz Thai fish sauce
20 long red chillies
A handful Thai basil, leaves picked

1. In a wok, heat the oil until smoking. Add the diced pork and stir fry for approximately 10 minutes until crisp all over. Drain half of the oil and reserve. Add the sugar and cook for 4–5 minutes to caramelize.

2. Add the soy and fish sauces. Bring back to the boil and remove from the heat and allow to cool. Transfer to a bowl, cover until required.

3. Roast the chillies in a large roasting tray with the reserved oil for 10 minutes and allow to cool. Do not de-seed or skin. Drain the chillies and reserve the oil.

4. To serve, place four chillies on each plate with a little bit of the reserved chilli oil and a large spoonful of sweet pork relish and a few Thai basil leaves.

121

Nam Phrik Ong

A local lady just outside Bangkok showed me how to make Nam Phrik Ong. The speed with which she peeled Thai shallots was enough to make me realize how little knowledge I really have of the Thai way of cooking. I guess that to have a complete understanding you must live in Thailand for several years and break away from your own culture.
Makes 150g/5¹/₂oz

5 dried chillies
2 small pieces galangal, peeled and chopped
5ml/1tsp salt
1 small onion, peeled and diced
5ml/1tsp shrimp paste
8 cloves garlic
100g/3¹/₂oz minced pork
60g/2oz sliced cherry tomatoes
50ml/2fl oz vegetable oil
a handful of coriander with roots

1. Soak the chillies in warm water for 15 minutes. Drain and place in a mortar and pestle with the galangal and salt. Pound until smooth, then add the onion and shrimp paste and pound again.
2. Add 5 cloves of garlic and pound with the pork. Finally, add the tomatoes, and pound and mix well. Chop the remaining garlic.

3. Heat the oil in a wok until hot and add the chopped garlic, fry for 1 minute until fragrant.
4. Add the prepared chilli paste and cook over a low heat for 5 minutes until coloured, then stir in the rest of the ingredients with 4 tsp water.
5. Taste and adjust seasoning and continue to cook for about 10 minutes until it thickens.

Sambal Blanchan

Like chilli jam, the form in which sambal comes is affected by the region it comes from. This sambal calls for large amounts of shrimp paste or blanchan, as it is known in Malaysia. The black thick resin is unsightly and the power of its smell is sometimes hard to handle. But once all the ingredients are added to it and it has been cooked, it is tasty. In fact Thais have a dish where the shrimp paste is first wrapped in banana leaf and then placed over a fire. It is cooked for 5 minutes on each side and then served as a dip with vegetables.
Makes 600g/1lb 5oz

5 dry chillies
10 fresh red chillies, de-seeded
5 fresh green chillies, de-seeded
30ml/2 tbsp vegetable oil
1 large onion, peeled and chopped
400g/14oz black blanchan (shrimp paste)
about 125ml/4fl oz lime juice

1. Place the dry chillies in a small saucepan and cover with water. Bring to the boil and simmer for 10 minutes until tender. Drain well and cool in cold water. Drain and remove the seeds. Pound or grind in a mortar along with the fresh chillies to form a coarse paste.
2. Heat the oil in a wok and fry the chopped onion and chilli paste for 2–3 minutes until fragrant. Remove with as little oil as possible into a bowl.
3. Cut the block of blanchan into thin slices and fry gently in the wok with as little oil as possible for 5 minutes till fragrant. Remove and add to fried chillies and onion.
4. Add lime juice to taste and mix well.

Nam Phrik Ong

Satay Sauce

In the street markets in and around Thailand, satay and grilled meat is very common. But the sauce, if any is served, will be sweet chilli, and not the peanut-based satay sauce we are more used to in the West. I've included it anyway as it is great to eat outside or indoors.
Makes 1litre/ 1³/₄ pt

250ml/7fl oz thick coconut cream
30ml/2 tbsp red curry paste (see page 97)
45ml/3 tbsp fish sauce
45ml/3 tbsp palm sugar
60ml/4 tbsp tamarind water
150g/5¹/₂oz roasted peanuts, chopped
600ml/1pt thin coconut milk

1. In a saucepan, combine the coconut cream and red curry paste and cook for 5 minutes over a low heat. Add the fish sauce, palm sugar, tamarind water and chopped peanuts. Cook for a further 5 minutes.
2. Add coconut milk.

Nam Jim

This is a very versatile salad dressing – I would call it the mother of all dressings. In Thailand, the ingredients will vary from place to place, and this recipe gives what is essentially a guideline for quantities. Again, this is a chance to learn by tasting until the right balance is achieved. You will know when this is – when the flavour makes you smile.
Makes 600ml/ 1pt

2 garlic cloves, peeled
3 coriander roots, cleaned
3 green small chillies
500ml/18fl oz fresh lime juice
45ml/3tbsp palm sugar
45ml/3tbsp fish sauce

1. Pound garlic and coriander roots lightly in a mortar – only one or two blows are necessary. Add the chillies and then the lime juice. Pound again.

2. Add the palm sugar and the fish sauce to taste. The flavour should be balanced – not salty, not garlic flavoured, not too sweet.

Sweet Chilli Sauce 1

The two recipes are adaptations of sweet chilli sauce. Sweet chilli is the main condiment used by Thais for street food; it usually comes in little plastic bags, sealed with rubber bands, convenient for pouring from or for dipping into.
Sauce1 makes 100ml/ 4fl oz
Sauce 2 makes 100ml/ 4fl oz

50ml/2fl oz coconut vinegar
50g/1³/₄ oz caster sugar
¹/₄ cucumber, sliced
¹/₄ cucumber, finely shredded
2 small red chillies, sliced
2 small green chillies, sliced

1. Heat the vinegar and sugar together with 2 tbsp water until boiling. Set aside to cool.
2. Mix all the ingredients together with the vinegar mixture and leave to sit for 15–20 minutes. Place in a bowl and serve.

Sweet Chilli Sauce 2

75ml/5 tbsp rice vinegar
75g/2¹/₂ oz sugar
3 long red chillies, de-seeded
20ml/4 tsp finely diced red chilli
20ml/4 tsp diced cucumber
10ml/2 tsp chopped peanuts

1. Place all the vinegar, sugar and de-seeded chillies in a large saucepan. Bring to the boil, simmer and cook for 15 minutes. Remove from the heat and cool for 10 minutes. Place in a food processor and sieve and leave to cool.
2. Stir in the diced chilli and serve sprinkled with diced cucumber and chopped peanuts.

Pad Phrik King

Served with Thai basil and shredded lime leaves, this is one of the most delicious and fiery of the Thai dishes in this book. Once again the recipe calls for huge quantities because it takes so long to cook – the paste keeps very well in the fridge. If pork fat is unavailable then you could use duck fat or vegetable oil at a push.

Makes 500g/1lb

100g/3½oz dried red chillies
200g/7oz red onions peeled
200g/7oz peeled garlic
60g/2oz galangal, peeled
20g/¾oz coriander root
60g/2oz dried red shrimps, rinsed and dried
60g/2oz lemon grass
200g/7oz pork fat for cooking
10ml/2 tsp palm sugar
2.5ml/½ tsp fish sauce

1. Place the dried chillies in a large bowl and cover with warm water. Leave to soak for 15 minutes. Drain and remove the seeds. In a food processor blend the onions, garlic, galangal, coriander, prawns and lemon grass together with the chilli until as smooth as possible.
2. In a saucepan, melt the pork fat. Add the prepared paste and cook for approximately 2 hours, on a low heat. Do be careful not to allow the bottom of the saucepan to catch.
3. Halfway through cooking, add half of the palm sugar and mix through thoroughly. Continue cooking slowly. When aromatic and deeper in colour, the taste should have a completely different flavour and be more palatable.
4. Add fish sauce. When cooked, remove from heat and cool, ready for use.

7

DESSERTS

Sweet things in Thailand come in three main categories; fresh fruit, confectionery and snacks. Large plates of fresh fruit usually grace the table at the end of a banquet: mangoes, bananas, papayas and pineapples, and if you are really lucky, huge pomelos served with tubs of salt mixed with brown sugar for dipping. Thai banquets are full of flavours and textures, but sweet flavours are considered a necessary part of the end of a meal.

Confectionery is eaten by many people at all times of the day and night and is made with great love and style. The masters of this art take their time, using many different cooking methods often learnt in the royal courts, because the wealthy were the only people able to afford them. Made with the finest young coconut milk and crystal clear sugar syrups, many are flavoured with the highly perfumed flowers of jasmine. These sweets take on many forms – from the very soft jellies to the bouncy ones which have been set with agar, a natural setting agent similar to gelatine, which is made from seaweed.

Sweet snacks are very rarely made in the home but are bought on street stalls and in the markets. These snacks are eaten as part of the daily food consumption and they are very sweet and rich. They are made up of vegetables and starches, and vary from sweet potato cooked in sugar syrup, to tapioca, sago and rice noodles steeped in sweet coconut milk, served warm with extra sugar poured over the top.

As it is so hot in the cities, many people sell bags of ice flavoured with sweet fruit syrups and fruit drinks made with anything from the smelly durian fruit to lychee juice. The ice is enough to give the people the sugar boost that is needed to survive in this kind of heat and means that those with a sweet tooth can get their kick at any time of the day rather than waiting until after a meal as we in the West tend to do.

Sweet Rice Noodle Salad with Palm Sugar

Sweet Rice Noodle Salad with Palm Sugar

Noodles are *the* snack food and this sweet version is no exception. Served in the street markets in the major cities and villages, you can choose your topping and then sit on the street corner and fill your belly.
Serves 4–6

300g/10½oz rice noodles
500ml/18fl oz coconut milk and fresh coconut milk to serve
200g/7oz palm sugar
10ml/2tsp salt
100g/3½oz palm sugar for grating
100g/3½oz roasted coconut (shavings)

1. Soak the rice noodles in water for an hour, then drain.
2. Pour the coconut milk into a saucepan and add the sugar and salt. Bring to the boil and add the rice noodles. Remove from the heat and leave to cool, then transfer to a serving bowl.
3. To serve, place a single portion of noodles in a bowl, warm in the microwave and turn out onto a plate. Coat with fresh coconut milk, grated palm sugar and roasted coconut.

Coconut Milk Ice Cream

This ice cream or frozen milk will have to be eaten as soon as it comes out of the freezer as it melts quickly. Serve with fresh fruit and roasted grated coconut.
Makes 1½/2¾ pt

250ml/9fl oz pure or scented water
1kg/2lb 4oz coconut, freshly grated
5 tsp sugar
250g/9oz Cantaloupe or honey-dew melon purée

1. Heat the water in a saucepan and add the coconut flesh. Remove from the heat and allow to cool until you are able to handle it. Then knead and squeeze the coconut to obtain approximately 750ml/1¾ pt of coconut milk.
2. Dissolve sugar and salt in the coconut milk. Add the melon purée and stir until well mixed.
3. Use an ice cream maker to churn this mixture into sorbet.

Caramelized Sweet Banana

The bananas we have become used to in the West are generally quite large and their bends may well have had to pass EEC standard regulations. In the land of smiles there are no silly laws like that. The bananas served are usually very small and are high in sugar and sometimes called sugar bananas. Thais, not quite content with the amount of sugar in the fruit, have to add more! The bananas for this recipe shouldn't be over-ripe otherwise they will become too soft and mushy.
Serves 8

250ml/9fl oz thick coconut milk
400g/14oz sugar
2.5ml/½ tsp salt
1 lime, juiced
8 small ripe bananas, peeled and cut into 2.5x5cm/1 x 2inch pieces
750ml/1¾ pt coconut water from young coconuts

1. Pour the coconut water into a saucepan and bring to the boil. Add the sugar, salt and lime juice and simmer until reduced to about 600ml/1 pt.
2. Place the pieces of banana in the syrup and continue to simmer for 5 minutes until banana is cooked.
3. In a saucepan reduce thick coconut milk with a pinch more salt quickly over heat. It should not separate. Use it as a topping for the sweetened banana pieces. Serve hot or cold.

Sago Pudding with Plums

Sago is to many a reminder of school days and generally just the thought of it is pretty much a no no. Combining the sago with plums changes all that – the acid in the fruit breaks down the sweetness and adds to the texture. The chalk in this recipe aids digestion and adds a gentle soft flavour.
Serves 4–6

Palm Sugar Syrup
600ml/1 pt water
325g/1½ oz sugar
1 vanilla pod, split lengthways
¼ lime

Poached Plums
675g/1½lb plums

Sago Pudding
300g/10½ oz sago flour
3litre/5¼ pt water
5ml/1tsp powdered white writing chalk
Freshly grated coconut and ½tsp salt to serve

1. First make the Palm Sugar Syrup. Combine all the ingredients in a large saucepan. Bring to the boil and set aside.
2. To make the poached plums, preheat the oven to 160°C/310°F/Gas 2. Quarter the plums or cut into sixes, depending on their size. Place in a roasting pan and pour the palm sugar syrup over the top of them.
3. Cover the roasting pan with foil, place in the oven and cook for 10 minutes. Remove from the oven and take off the foil. Set aside to cool to room temperature.
4. To make the Sago Pudding, combine the sago flour, water and chalk; mix well. Strain through a fine sieve into a heavy-bottomed pan. Bring to the boil, then simmer for about 30 minutes, stirring occasionally until the mixture thickens.
5. Mix half the plums with the sago pudding and serve with the remaining plums and grated coconut.

Lychee and Ginger Water Ice

Big bags of ice flavoured with fruit syrups are so refreshing and the thought of cooling down by sucking shaves of flavoured ice on a hot day makes me go weak at the knees. This is a simple recipe and when the lychees are in season they are cheap.
Serves 4–6

300g/10½oz fresh lychees
200g/7oz sugar
Juice of 1 lime
150ml/¼pt water
15g/½oz grated root ginger

1. Peel the lychees and place them in a saucepan with the sugar and the lime juice. Pour over 100ml/3½ fl oz of water and bring to the boil.
2. Cook the lychees for 4 minutes, remove from the heat and allow to cool.
3. When cool, remove the seeds from the fruit and purée the flesh with the remaining ingredients.
4. Place in an ice cream maker, churn and freeze or place in large thin trays and freeze, stirring occasionally, until solid.

Fresh Fruit with Mint Jelly
Makes 20

Mint Jelly
500g/1lb 2oz sugar
200ml/7fl oz water
100ml/3½fl oz lemon juice
1 bunch mint, washed
4 leaves gelatine
1 bunch chopped mint

Fruit Plate
2 mangoes
1 punnet of raspberries or strawberries
2 bananas
1 pineapple
4 lychees

1. First, make the jelly in a saucepan. Bring the sugar, water and lemon juice to the boil. Add mint. Take off the stove and leave to infuse.
2. Strain, add gelatine then chopped mint and place in fridge until set.
3. When ready to serve, prepare all the fruit and arrange on plates. Serve with a scoop of mint jelly.

Fresh Fruit

Coconut Jelly

Coconut jelly comes in little squares and these are packed in plastic boxes and sold from the Thai sweet stalls or supermarkets. It is usually made in two layers, one of pure white coconut and the other is green, taking the flavour and colour of the pandan leaf. If you split the mixture in two parts and crush the pandan in one half and leave for one hour, it will take on a green hue.
Makes 250g/9oz

200ml/7fl oz water
1 l/1³/4 pt coconut milk
10 leaves gelatine
1 young coconut

1. In a large saucepan, bring the water and coconut milk to the boil and skim off any fat. Make sure you still have 1litre/1³/4 pt of liquid. If not, boil further to reduce or add more water to make up to 1 litre.
2. Put the gelatine leaves in a bowl of cold water to re-hydrate. Remove them from the water and squeeze to remove excess water.
3. Put the gelatine in a fine sieve and pour the hot liquid over the top of the gelatine. Set aside to cool.
4. Cut the young coconut in half, then with a spoon, remove the flesh and finely shred.
5. When the coconut milk has cooled, stir the coconut shreds in to the mixture and leave to set in the fridge for 12 hours.
6. To serve, cut the coconut mix into cubes and serve with fruit.

Typical Thai confectionery – coconut and pandan jelly

Deep Fried Bananas
Serves: 3–4

100g/3½oz rice flour
Pinch of salt
100g/3½oz fresh coconut grated
50g/2oz granulated sugar
1 tbsp sesame seeds
125ml/4fl oz water
Vegetable oil for deep frying
5 sugar or ladies fingers (small, sweet) bananas, peeled
100ml/3½fl oz thin coconut milk to serve
100g/3½oz palm sugar, melted to serve

1. Sift the flour with the salt into a bowl.
2. Stir in the coconut, sugar and sesame seeds and whisk in the water. Allow to stand for 5 minutes. The batter should be of a consistency to coat the bananas easily. If it is too thick add another 30ml/2 tbsp of water.
3. Heat the oil for deep frying. Dip into the batter and deep fry, a few at a time for 5–6 minutes until golden.
4. Remove, drain and serve immediately. To serve, pour coconut milk on a plate, stack on top with bananas and drizzle with the melted palm sugar.

Steamed Sticky Rice and Banana or Mango

Sticky rice cooked with huge quantities of sugar is a common snack served on roadside stalls in Thailand. Once the art of the rolling is mastered, they will become a standard feature at your parties and picnics. Fill with mango or you can eat the sweetened rice porridge with fresh fruit as it is.
Serves 4

250g/9oz white sticky rice
90ml/6tbsp black sticky rice
50g/1¾oz caster sugar
2 bananas
150ml/¼pt coconut milk, homemade or canned
½ tsp salt
2 banana leaves
150g/5 oz palm sugar

1. Using separate bowls of cold water, soak the black rice for three hours and the white rice for 1 hour, drain. Line a steamer tray or a colander with a cloth and place the black rice inside. Sprinkle with 2 tbsps of the sugar. Cover and steam over boiling water for 30–40 minutes until just tender. Repeat with the white rice, sprinkling it with 4 tbsps of the sugar and steaming for 25–30 minutes.
2. Peel and halve the bananas. Place the coconut milk, remaining 50g/1¾oz sugar and salt in a saucepan and bring to a boil, stirring. Add the bananas and cook for 3 minutes. Remove from the heat. Allow to cool in the milk, then remove with a slotted spoon, reserving the cooking liquid.
3. Cut 30cm/12 inch squares from the two banana leaves. Cut one of the squares into four smaller pieces, about 15 x 10cm /6 x 4inches. Blanch the leaves in boiling water for 20 seconds. Drain and dry with paper towels.
4. Lay one of the larger squares on a flat surface and place a smaller piece of leaf diagonally in the centre. Spread 1 tbsp of white rice over the smaller square, leaving a 1cm/½inch border all round. Cover with thin layer of black rice, and place half a banana on top.
5. Cover with another layer of black rice, and then a top layer of white rice, and drizzle with 1 tbsp of the reserved cooking liquid.
6. Take two opposite corners of the larger piece of leaf, bring them together and roll them down, one over the other, wrapping the rice tightly inside. Fold the remaining two corners over this fold and turn the parcel over so that all the tucks are underneath. Repeat with the remaining leaves.
7. Steam the parcels for 25 minutes until tender.
8. Gently melt the palm sugar in a small pan, taking care not to let it boil as this will spoil the flavour.
9. To serve, cut the parcels in half just off the diagonal. Place one half on top of the other on individual plates. Drizzle with a little more of the reserved cooking liquid and spoon over the melted sugar.

Deep Fried Bananas

Contributors' Information

Thai Airways Reservations
London: 0171 499 9113
Manchester: 0161 831 7861

Thai Airways International London to Bangkok
non-stop service departs every morning, with
additional evening services on Tuesday,
Thursday and Saturday, for easy connections
throughout South-East Asia or to any of
Thai's 22 destinations throughout Thailand.

Thai Airways offer complimentary
drinks, delicious cuisine and a comprehensive
in-flight entertainment programme. 'A
gracious welcome, a fresh orchid, a unique
blend of tradition and technology.'

Thai Airways International's service
really is smooth as silk.

Bangkok Airways
For information on Bangkok Airways contact
The Tourism Authority of Thailand
Tel: 0870 900 2007

Reservations can be made through any international carrier or once you arrive in Thailand
at the Bangkok Airways booking desks.

Bangkok Airways is the major carrier
operating throughout the day, seven days a
week between Bangkok and Ko Samui as well
as connecting other areas of Thailand, such as
Sukothai, Chiang Mai, Pattaya and Phuket.
The new Samui Express operates a bi-weekly
link between Singapore and Ko Samui.

Check with any Swiss Air office for
availability of 'Samui Plus' passes which allow
for discounted multi-stops around Thailand.

Eastern and Oriental Express
Brochure Line: 01233 211 772
Reservations: 0171 805 5100
Website: www.orient-expresstrains.com

A year-round service of 2 nights and 3 days
operates between Singapore and Bangkok via
the Malay Peninsula and costs from £800 per
person which includes all breakfasts, served by
your Compartment Steward in your cabin,
lunch, tea and dinner.

If you do not feel you can appreciate the
changing landscape from the comfort of the
open observation car or your cabin, optional
sight-seeing tours are included in the cost.

There are also some over-night
departures between Bangkok and Chiang Mai
starting at £490.

The train really is the epitome of luxury
and decadence with beautiful bars serving
Champagne in crystal glasses, elegant dining-
cars and ensuite sleeping compartments.
Dress is refined yet relaxed during the day
and glamour and style is encouraged during
the evening, when passengers dine on an
Euro-Asian menu prepared by Chef de
Cuisine Kevin Cape.

Mandarin Oriental Hotel Group Reservations
Tel: 0800 962667

This luxury hotel group also owns hotels in
Hawaii, Hong Kong, Jakarta, Kuala Lumpur,
London, Macau, Manila, San Francisco,
Singapore and Surabaya.

The Oriental Hotel – Bangkok
48 Oriental Avenue
Bangkok 10500
Tel: 66 22 36 0400-20
Fax: 66 24 39 7587

The Oriental, located on the river in Bangkok for over 120 years, is one of the premier hotels in the area, where staff outnumber guests by two to one. All the rooms are opulent with huge ensuite bathrooms and a personal butler service. For a special occasion it may be worth upgrading to the Author's Wing, named after guests such as Joseph Conrad, Noël Coward or Somerset Maugham.

Superior rooms start at US$250 per night, with Author's suites at US$880.

The Oriental Thai Cooking School

Since opening its doors fifteen years ago, the school has taught thousands of people from all over the world the art of Thai cuisine. Classes of a maximum of fifteen people can be taken as one-off day courses or a complete course divided as follows:-

Monday: introduction, ingredients, snacks and salads
Tuesday: soups, desserts, fruit and vegetable carvings
Wednesday: curries, condiments and side-dishes
Thursday: Steam, stir fry, fry and grill menu preparations

The cooking school is open to everyone, from guests at the hotel to Bangkok residents and costs from US$120 per person per class.

Alternatively, The Oriental offers a five night hotel/cookery school package including:-
■ limousine transport to and from Bangkok Airport
■ welcome dinner at the Sala Rim Naam Restaurant
■ Jet Lag Massage at The Oriental Spa
■ five nights' bed and breakfast in a superior room
■ cookery classes including lunch on Monday, Wednesday and Friday
Prices start at US$1,788 per person.

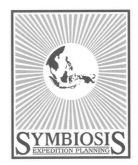

Symbiosis Expedition Planning
205 St John's Hill
London, SW11 1TH
Tel: 0171 924 5906
Fax: 0171 924 5907
Website: www.symbiosis-travel.co.uk
E-mail: Info@Symbiosis-travel.co.uk

Symbiosis arranges tailor-made expeditions by helping the individual to choose a set of travel locations and goals and giving the advice and support needed to achieve them. This begins before the trip as they organise visas, tickets and accommodation and actually throughout your tour as they put you in touch with local operators and English-speaking guides.

Symbiosis took us from Bangkok to The Thai House and then helped us through the northern leg of the journey from Chiang Mai, into hill-tribes and jungle.

A typical 15 day expedition called 'A Feast of Thailand' introduces the country and its cuisine, giving the traveller the chance to experience some hands-on cooking as well as relax and appreciate the culture. Beginning in Bangkok and travelling through Chiang-Mai, Chiang Rai and the Golden Triangle, this particular tour costs from £995 and includes all board, food and travel except international flights.

Symbiosis also organize expeditions around Malaysia, Indonesia, the Philippines, Vietnam, Laos, Cambodia and Papua New Guinea.

THE THAI HOUSE

The Thai House
Reservations Tel: 66 22 2800 740
Fax: 66 22 2800 741
Or contact Symbiosis Expedition Planning

This traditional Ayuthaya-style teakwood house is a real Thai home situated 40 minutes by boat outside Bangkok. The owners will welcome you into their home and treat you as a guest and friend rather than a customer. Here you will be introduced to real Thai customs and food in a relaxing and informal way.

The rooms are in traditional style with the extra comforts of fans, mattresses and Western toilet and showering facilities. The Thai House also offers a cookery course, run by the owner, which explains the importance of food and mealtimes in the Thai day and gives the guest a chance to experience the excitement of an early morning market as well as the preparation and eating of the food.

Westin Chiang Mai
318/1 Chiang Mai
Lumphun Road
Wat Katte, Muang
Chiang Mai 50000
Tel: 66 53 275 300
Fax: 6653 275 299
Westin Reservations line:
0800 282 565
Or contact Symbiosis Expedition Planning

THE WESTIN CHIANGMAI

This quality business hotel is a great stop-over destination in Chiang Mai, only 10 minutes from the airport and close to the business and shopping areas of Chiang Mai. Its 526 rooms overlook the Ping River and as you would expect from a business hotel, all rooms have the usual air-con, colour TV and direct-dial telephones.

The River Terrace restaurant is famed for its intricately carved fruit and vegetables that decorate the authentic Thai meals served.

Room rates vary according to the time of year and offers are often available but at the time of filming a double room started at £81 on a room only basis. Call the international reservations line for up to date information.

Track of the Tiger Tours
and Maekok River Lodge
P.O.BOX 3
Mae Ai
Chiang Mai 50280
Thailand
Tel: 66 53 459 328
Fax: 66 53 459 329
Website: www.track-of-the-tiger
E-Mail: tiger@loxinfo.co.th

Located close to the Thai-Burma border and overlooking the giant Buddha image of this temple on the opposite bank of the river, the wooden lodge blends perfectly with the landscape and offers a high level of Thai cuisine. Soft adventure tours can be arranged including a visit to local hill-tribe villages, elephant trekking or a trip up river by raft to the river base camp to experience life in the jungle and campfire fun. These tours are suitable for accompanied children.

At the Markok River Lodge a single room costs 850 baht per night and a double 950 baht (approximately £13.50 and £15 respectively). Prices for the various tours are available by visiting the website, contacting Track of the Tiger direct or booking through Symbiosis Expedition Planning in the UK.

Laem Set Inn
110 mu 2, Hua Thanon
Ko Samui, Surat Thani, 84310
Thailand
Tel: 00 66 77 424393
Fax: 00 66 77 424 394
Website: www.laemset.com
E-mail: inn@laemset.com

Laem Set Inn is located on the island of Ko Samui off the south-east coast of Thailand. The resort is almost at the southernmost tip of the island in a very secluded and peaceful spot well away from the main tourist developments.

The combination of wooden Thai bungalows, air-conditioned rooms and suites amoungst the palm trees creates a tropical village atmosphere. Each one has its own balcony and view of the sea. The whole place has a wonderfully relaxed atmosphere and is a perfect place to dive and snorkel on the beautiful coral reef, sunbathe and swim, or explore the local islands by boat.

Tasting Places
Unit 40, Buspace Studios
Conlan Street
London, W10 5AP
Tel: 0171 460 0077
Fax: 0171 460 0029
Website: www.tastingplaces.com
Email: ss@tastingplaces.com
The cookery holiday featured in the series hosted by chef Paul Blain was taken with Tasting Places. A week's holiday including all classes, accommodation, food and wine starts at £1,200.
For 2000 dates and other cookery holiday destinations call Tasting Places or visit their website.

For the last 7 years, Tasting Places has been organizing 'hands on' cookery holidays at stunning locations in Italy for people who love and appreciate fine food and wine. Their recent addition of Thai courses are proving just as popular and new locations around the world are planned for next year.

Chefs for 1999 include Alistair Little, Ross Burden, Thane Prince and Peter Gordon.

Paul Blain

Paul Blain started his Thai Cooking in Sydney with David Thompson at the Darley Street Thai, one of Australia's most renowned Thai restaurants. After many trips and much research, he opened his highly acclaimed restaurant The Chilli Jam Café in Noosa, Queensland. Paul is now opening his new Thai cookery school and Asian market garden in Queensland. His enthusiasm is inspiring and infectious.

Thanks to Paul for contributing both his Roasted Chilli Paste recipe and his Spicy Soup of Smoked Fish and Coconut to the book.

Muji Field Cooker
For your nearest store or stockist call:
0171 323 2208

Our faithful old field cooker came from Muji and is available at a cost of £95. We found it really versatile, you can literally cook in any way from barbecues to steaming to wokking to smoking and it all fits inside the metal drum for easy transportation.

For more information on holidays in Thailand, contact the Tourism Authority of Thailand brochure line on 0870 900 2007.

141